CITYSPOTS
ZAGREB

D0802724

WHAT'S IN YOUR GUIDEBOOK?

Independent authors Impartial up-to-date information from our travel experts who meticulously source local knowledge.

Experience Thomas Cook's 165 years in the travel industry and guidebook publishing enriches every word with expertise you can trust.

Travel know-how Thomas Cook has thousands of staff working around the globe, all living and breathing travel.

Editors Travel-publishing professionals, pulling everything together to craft a perfect blend of words, pictures, maps and design.

You, the traveller We deliver a practical, no-nonsense approach to information, geared to how you really use it.

CITYSPOTS
ZAGREB

Written by Tony Kelly
Updated by Gorana Nad-Conlan

Published by Thomas Cook Publishing
A division of Thomas Cook Tour Operations Limited
Company registration No: 3772199 England
The Thomas Cook Business Park, 9 Coningsby Road
Peterborough PE3 8SB, United Kingdom
Email: books@thomascook.com, Tel: +44 (0)1733 416477
www.thomascookpublishing.com

Produced by The Content Works Ltd
Aston Court, Kingsmead Business Park, Frederick Place
High Wycombe, Bucks HP11 1LA
www.thecontentworks.com

Series design based on an original concept by Studio 183 Limited

ISBN: 978-1-84848-139-8

First edition © 2007 Thomas Cook Publishing
This second edition © 2009 Thomas Cook Publishing
Text © Thomas Cook Publishing
Maps © Thomas Cook Publishing/PCGraphics (UK) Limited
Transport map © Communicarta Limited

Series Editor: Lucy Armstrong
Production/DTP: Steven Collins

Printed and bound in Spain by GraphyCems

Cover photography (Tkalčićeva) © In Depth Imagery/Alamy

CONTENTS

CITYSPOTS

SYMBOLS KEY

The following symbols are used throughout this book:

ⓐ address ⓣ telephone ⓦ website address ⓔ email
ⓛ opening times ⓝ public transport connections ⓘ important

The following symbols are used on the maps:

🄸	information office	▪	points of interest
✈	airport	⭕	city
✚	hospital	◯	large town
🛡	police station	○	small town
🚏	bus station	═	motorway
🚆	railway station	—	main road
✝	cathedral		minor road
❶	numbers denote	—	railway
	featured cafés & restaurants		

Hotels and restaurants are graded by approximate price as follows:
£ budget price ££ mid-range price £££ expensive

▷ *A lion monument at the Mirogoj Cemetery*

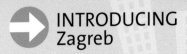

Introduction

Zagreb is a Central European city with a Mediterranean attitude. Take a seat at a grand old coffee house or spend a night at the opera and you could be in 19th-century Vienna, but wander the streets at midnight on a summer evening and the *joie de vivre* of the inhabitants might remind you of Barcelona or Rome.

Centuries of foreign rule by Vienna, Budapest and Belgrade have left their mark on everything from architecture to cuisine. Since 1991, however, Zagreb has finally fulfilled its destiny as the proud capital of an independent Croatia and home to one in four of the country's population. The distinctive red-and-white chequerboard of the Croatian flag flies from government buildings and the iconic statue of nationalist hero Josip Jelačić, dismantled when the city was part of Communist Yugoslavia, once again dominates the main square.

Yet, despite their understandable pride in their new nation, the people of Zagreb look outward to the rest of the world – and to a European Union which Croatia is hoping to join by 2011. Most young people speak excellent English, a result not only of education but also of years of exposure to foreign films, music and TV. Many families fled abroad during the dark days of Communism and the wars of the 1990s, returning from the UK, US and Australia with entrepreneurial vision and new ideas.

This openness to outsiders is only part of what makes Zagreb such a welcoming and friendly place to visit. It has great restaurants and cafés, peaceful parks for strolling, colourful markets, buzzing nightlife and a vibrant cultural scene. Despite this, Zagreb has so far managed to avoid the tourist crowds that have almost overwhelmed other former Eastern Bloc cities such as Prague, Krakow and Budapest. Go now to discover the secret before everyone else does.

● *The café culture is all part of Zagreb's appeal*

When to go

Zagreb has a typically Central European climate, with mild summers and cold winters. Spring is a pleasant time to visit, with temperatures rising to 18°C (64°F) by late May – though May and June are also the wettest months. Summer is hot and sultry, reaching over 30°C (86°F) in July and August, though it is usually several degrees cooler on the summit of Medvednica. From mid-June to mid-September the city is strangely quiet, as everyone heads for the coast and theatres and nightclubs close their doors for the summer. There is plenty of open-air entertainment, though, and the terrace bars and cafés are always busy.

September is a lovely month, as Zagreb comes back to life with the arrival of the students and it is still warm enough to sit out of doors. Autumn brings pretty colours to the parks, but also wet, windy weather and chilly nights. Winter (see pages 14–15) is a very special time in Zagreb, but don't forget to wrap up warm as average temperatures rarely rise above 0°C (32°F) in December and January.

ANNUAL EVENTS
Spring
St Mark's Festival (April) Held around the time of St Mark's Day (25 April), this features two weeks of classical concerts in St Mark's Church. ⓦ www.festivalsvmarka.hr

Summer
Cest is d'Best (June) Zagreb becomes the backdrop to street performers from near and far. Bump into bands, buskers,

jugglers and alternative thesps in and around the main square.
 www.kraljeviulice.com

INMusic festival (June/early July) This two-day annual event at
Šalata attracts such big-name acts as Nick Cave & The Bad Seeds,
The Prodigy and Hot Chip.  www.inmusicfestival.com

▲ *Autumnal hues in Zagreb's Botanical Garden*

Zagreb Summer Evenings (July–early August) Orchestral and chamber music and organ concerts in the cathedral and St Catherine's Church are counterpoised by blues and jazz gigs. Ⓦ www.kdz.hr

International Folklore Festival (mid-July) Founded in 1966 and still going strong, this festival presents folk singers and dancers on an open-air stage in Trg bana Jelačića. Look out for groups from Slavonia, eastern Croatia, performing the *kolo* (circle dance) to the sound of the *tamburica* (mandolin). Ⓦ www.msf.hr

PIF (International Puppet Theatre Festival) (late August/early September) This week-long festival is always a big hit with kids, as puppeteers from across Europe take over the city's streets, squares and theatres. The festival has been going for 40 years. Ⓦ www.mcuk.hr

Autumn

Zagreb World Theatre Festival (September) Contemporary drama from around the world performed at the Croatian National Theatre. Ⓦ www.zagrebtheatrefestival.hr

Zagreb International Autumn Fair (September) The biggest trade fair in the region includes an 'eco-ethno' fair of Croatian produce and crafts. Businessmen flock to the city and hotel prices go up, so check out the dates and avoid this week if you can. Ⓦ www.zv.hr

Hrvatski Jazz Sabor (Croatian Jazz Assembly) (late September/early October) Held at the legendary BP Club (see page 92), this two-week festival features live jazz every night from Boško Petrović and friends. Ⓦ www.bpclub.hr

Queer Zagreb (October) Zagreb's gay and lesbian scene has been slow to take off, but this annual gay arts festival has five days of cinema, drama, music and dance at venues across the city. ⓦ www.queerzagreb.org

Zagreb Film Festival (October) International directors compete for the Golden Pram awards for best new documentary, feature film and short film over five days of movie mania at the Student Centre on Savska. ⓦ www.zagrebfilmfestival.com

Winter
Advent in the Heart of Zagreb Come for Christmas markets, mulled wine and concerts in Trg bana Jelačića (see pages 14–15).

PUBLIC HOLIDAYS
New Year's Day 1 Jan
Epiphany 6 Jan
Easter Sunday 4 Apr 2010; 24 Apr 2011; 15 Apr 2012
Easter Monday 5 Apr 2010; 25 Apr 2011; 16 Apr 2012
May Day 1 May
Corpus Christi 3 June 2010; 23 June 2011; 7 June 2012
Anti-Fascist Resistance Day 22 June
Croatian National Day 25 June
Homeland Victory Day 5 Aug
Assumption 15 Aug
Croatian Independence Day 8 Oct
All Saints' Day 1 Nov
Christmas Day 25 Dec

Christmas in Zagreb

Hawkers selling roast chestnuts from street-corner carts. Zrinjevac Park covered in a light dusting of snow. Christmas shoppers in warm coats sipping hot chocolate in cosy cafés. The New Year's Eve ball at the Esplanade Hotel. Skiing on Sljeme. Mulled wine and sausages. The city turned into a festival of lights. In many ways, winter in Zagreb is the most magical and romantic time of all.

In the weeks leading up to Christmas, the streets around Trg bana Jelačića become a sprawling outdoor market, with stalls selling decorations, food and handmade crafts. Florists are busy from morning to night making garlands, wreaths and arrangements for the Christmas table. Another popular gift is a *licitarsko srce*, a gingerbread heart flavoured with honey and pepper and decorated with coloured icing, traditionally given by sweethearts as a love token.

After dark, everyone gathers on the main square, where a tall Christmas tree is set up beside an open-air stage, and giant Advent candles illuminate the Manduševac fountain. Not just one but three different Santas (including one by the name of Grandpa Frost) take children for rides on trams and miniature trains. Later in the evening, there is a concert on the stage – maybe jazz, salsa or a children's choir. The musicians are wrapped up in hats, scarves and gloves to keep out the cold, while the audience stay warm by snuggling together, eating hot dogs with lashings of mustard and drinking hot wine out of plastic cups.

The temperature may be below freezing, but nothing can chill the spirit of the people of Zagreb. Winter is supposed to be cold, they say, but why should that stop them from enjoying life on the streets? As the music ends and everyone waits for their tram home, adults and children alike greet each other with the familiar words *Sretan Božić* (Happy Christmas).

🔺 *Roast chestnuts provide winter warmth*

History

The recorded history of Zagreb begins in 1094, when King Ladislas of Hungary founded a bishopric at Kaptol, on the site of today's cathedral. In 1242, King Bela of Hungary established the free and royal city of Gradec on a wooded hill across the Medveščak stream from Kaptol. The twin cities grew up side by side, each surrounded by walls and towers. There were frequent skirmishes between the two. After one particularly fierce battle, the bridge linking Gradec to Kaptol was christened Krvavi Most (Bloody Bridge), a name still in use today.

⬤ *The Arts & Crafts Museum is a fine example of 19th-century architecture*

Croatia acknowledged the Habsburg crown in 1527 and for the next 400 years Zagreb was an outpost of the Austro-Hungarian empire. It was only in 1850 that Gradec and Kaptol were officially united by imperial decree as the city of Zagreb. Rapid expansion followed, as Harmica (now Trg bana Jelačića) grew from a fairground and marketplace into the city square and Donji grad (Lower town) was laid out as a grid of avenues, parks and squares. An earthquake in 1880 destroyed much of the city, but the rebuilding produced some of the finest architecture in Zagreb, including the railway station, Arts & Crafts Museum and Croatian National Theatre.

The 20th century was not kind to Croatia. With the collapse of the Habsburg empire after World War I, Croatia became part of the kingdom of Yugoslavia. During World War II, Zagreb became the capital of the Independent State of Croatia, a Nazi puppet regime that carried out mass murders of Jews and Serbs. In 1945, Tito, whose father was Croatian, came to power across Yugoslavia, and Croatia became one of six socialist republics joined together in 'brotherhood and unity'.

Tito's brand of Communism was not always popular, but he held the country together for 35 years. After his death, Yugoslavia fell apart. Croatia declared independence in 1991 and for the next four years it defended itself in a vicious Homeland War against the Serbs. Although Zagreb was relatively unscathed, the presidential palace was attacked and thousands of volunteers went off to the front, leaving many people dead and emotional scars that have still not healed. Despite the turmoil of the 1990s, Zagreb is now looking towards a happier future and has recreated itself as a buzzing, 21st-century city.

Lifestyle

It would be easy to get the impression that the inhabitants of Zagreb spend all their time drinking coffee. There is nothing the average *Purger* (citizen of Zagreb) likes better than to sit outside a café with friends, reading the papers and discussing politics and sport. Saturday morning coffee on Trg bana Jelačića is the social highlight of the week and even the president has been known to join in. Although living standards are rising, most people still cannot afford to eat out; but they can sit on the terrace all morning for the price of a macchiato.

At night, everyone joins the *korzo*, the ritual promenade so beloved of Mediterranean countries, whose purpose is to see and be seen. Most young people are very fashion-conscious and the women dress to kill. The writer Adolf Hudovski captured the atmosphere in 1892 in the very first guidebook to Zagreb. 'In the morning, the bustle of the fair and the picturesque costumes of

THE GREAT OUTDOORS

Most *Purgeri* are passionate about the outdoor life and take every opportunity to escape the city for exercise and fresh air. On Sunday afternoons, they go hiking on Medvednica or take the family for a picnic in Maksimir Park. During the summer, Zagreb virtually empties as everyone heads for the Adriatic coast, while those who stay behind cool off by swimming in the lakes at Bundek and Jarun.

● *Catching up over a coffee*

the peasantry, and in the evening, during the promenade, a goodly number of Zagreb beauties are to be seen,' he wrote. A word of warning, however, for the guys. Although you will be swept off your feet by the beauty of Croatian women, the locals say that you will fall in love and be heartlessly rejected at least three times during your visit.

It's easy to get chatting to locals, but while most people are approachable and speak good English, some subjects are best avoided. Memories of the war are still fresh, and though people may want to talk about it and the trials of alleged war criminals in The Hague, it is better to listen politely than to blunder in with your own views.

Culture

Zagreb has a rich cultural tradition going back to the 19th century, when the Habsburg aristocracy would visit the city's theatres to see the first plays and operas in Croatian. The arts continue to play a major role in public life, with theatres, concert halls, museums and galleries putting on a varied programme of activities throughout the year.

As soon as you arrive, go to the tourist office on Trg bana Jelačića to pick up a copy of the monthly English-language *Events & Performances*. Then take a seat at a café and decide what you want to see. Tickets can sometimes be bought by telephone or online, but are generally cheaper if purchased one or two days in advance from the relevant box office. If you want to work out your schedule before you go, the listings are also available on the internet at ⓦ www.zagreb-touristinfo.hr

The prestigious venue for drama, ballet and opera is the Croatian National Theatre (see page 93), an ostentatious, Viennese-style opera house. Home to the National Ballet and National Opera, its repertoire includes everything from Shakespeare to Greek tragedy and Croatian Renaissance drama to *Swan Lake*. Plays are generally performed in Croatian, while opera is sung in the original language. Even if you don't understand the words, it is worth spending an evening here just for the atmosphere and to see inside the theatre. A seat in a box or on the balcony costs only a few pounds and you can always leave at the interval if you get bored. There is no strict dress code, but the locals like to dress up and you will definitely feel out of place if you turn up for the opera in a scruffy t-shirt and

The splendid ostentation of the Croatian National Theatre

jeans. The same applies to concerts at the Croatian Music Institute (see page 93) and Vatroslav Lisinski Concert Hall (see page 104), home of the Zagreb Philharmonic Orchestra.

If you would like to see something in English, the English Language Theatre of Zagreb held its première in 2005 and puts on occasional performances at the Mala Scena Theatre on Medveščak (see page 75).

The season for serious drama and opera runs from late September to June. During the summer months, Zagreb's cultural life moves out of doors, with Saturday morning promenade concerts at the bandstand in Zrinjevac Park and music and drama on the Amadeo summer stage in the courtyard of the Arts & Crafts Museum. This is also the time to hear baroque and classical music in the city's churches.

Finally, don't forget Zagreb's museums and art galleries. Not only are some of them works of art in themselves, they also put on thought-provoking temporary exhibitions by contemporary Croatian artists.

◗ *Rich in culture: the interior of the Croatian National Theatre*

Shopping

Although Zagreb is unlikely ever to rival Milan in the fashion stakes, the city has come a long way since the era of drab, state-run department stores with rows of empty shelves. These days, you can choose from traditional markets, modern shopping malls, and a growing number of delicatessens and stylish boutiques.

Good buys include Croatian wines and spirits, olive oil, honey, Istrian truffles, Samobor mustard and natural cosmetics made from Hvar lavender and Adriatic herbs. Other popular souvenirs are embroidery, Pag lace, gingerbread hearts and football shirts emblazoned with the red-and-white chequerboard of Croatia.

One popular fashion item which originated in Croatia is the men's tie, modelled on the silk scarves worn by Croatian officers in France during the Thirty Years War. The style came to be known as dressing *à la croate*, later corrupted to *cravate*. Silk ties, scarves and cravats are produced by the Croata company in Zagreb and sold in the Oktogon Arcade on Ilica (see page 87).

Ilica is the main shopping street, which runs west from

TAX REFUNDS

If you are buying something expensive, look for the Tax Free Shopping logo and ask for form PDV-P, which allows foreign nationals to reclaim a percentage of VAT (sales tax) on items over 500 kn. If you leave Croatia within three months, you can present the receipt, tax form and unwrapped goods at the border for authorisation of your refund.

Trg bana Jelačića for more than 2 km (over 1 mile). Croatian high-street fashion chains such as Heruc Galerija and Image Haddad are found close to the main square, but the further you go along Ilica, the more it shows remnants of its Communist past. For a funkier selection of boutiques, head south along Frankopanska or check out Tkalčićeva, north of Trg bana Jelačića.

⬥ *Floral delights at Dolac*

Zagreb's markets offer superb fresh produce and also provide a splash of local colour. The biggest and most central is Dolac (see page 71) but there are also farmers' markets at Britanski trg on Ilica and Branimirova, near the bus station. Alternatively, pick up a bargain at the Sunday morning antiques market on Britanski trg (see page 87). Unlike shops, where prices are fixed, in markets you can haggle to your heart's content.

USEFUL SHOPPING PHRASES

What time do the shops open/close?
Kada se zatvaraju otvaraju/trgovine?
Ka-da se 'zat-va-ra-yoo ot-va-ra-yoo/tr-'go-vine?

How much is this?
Koliko je to?
'Ko-li-ko ye to?

Can I try this on?
Mogu li to probati?
Mo-goo li to 'pro-ba-ti?

My size is ...
Moj broj je...
Moy broy ye...

I'll take this one, thank you
Hvala, uzet ću ovo
Hva-la, oo-zet choo o-vo

This is too large/too small/too expensive.
Do you have any others?
Ovo je preveliko/premalo/preskupo. Imate li nešto drugo?
O-vo ye 'pre-ve-li-ko/'pre-ma-lo/'pre-skoo-po. 'I-ma-te li ne-shto droo-go?

Eating & drinking

Croatian cuisine is a blend of Central European and Mediterranean influences, with the Balkan-style grilled meats and paprika-flavoured stews of the interior balanced by the lighter, healthier fare of the Adriatic coast and dishes such as pasta and risotto imported from Italy.

Most people eat lunch between 12.00 and 15.00, and dinner between 19.00 and 22.00, but restaurants stay open throughout the day and reservations are rarely necessary. Another popular option is brunch; usually a cheap, hearty bowl of goulash or bean stew, served between 10.00 and 14.00.

One dish you should definitely try is *ćevapčići* (grilled meatballs), which originates in Bosnia but is popular across the Balkans. Usually eaten as a fast-food snack with raw onions and crusty bread, it is best accompanied by *ajvar*, a spicy aubergine and pepper relish.

Other popular standbys are *grah* (bean soup, sometimes with sausage added, served at mountain huts on Medvednica), *janjetina* (spit-roast lamb) and *zagrebački odrezak* (Zagreb-style veal cutlet, stuffed with ham and cheese).

Vegetarians might have a hard time, though pizza and pasta

PRICE CATEGORIES
The symbols indicate the average cost of a three-course meal, excluding drinks.
£ up to 100 kn ££ 100–150 kn £££ over 150 kn

● Pastries to die for

are reliable choices. Salads are always listed separately on the menu as side dishes. Beware of innocuous-sounding vegetable dishes: they may have meat added, so check before you order. Ivica i Marica (see page 73) does good vegetarian food.

Desserts rarely go beyond *palačinke* (pancakes), so save your appetite and go to a *slastičarnica* (cake shop) for pastries and ice cream. Coffee after the meal is usually espresso, though you can order the full range of Italian-style coffees such as cappuccino and macchiato.

Croatia produces some excellent wines, especially in the regions of Dalmatia, Istria and Slavonia. White wines to look out for include Malvazija from Istria and Graševina from Slavonia. The best red wines are Dingač and Plavac Mali from southern Dalmatia. Portugizac is a light, fruity red produced close to Samobor, drunk in autumn straight after the harvest. The better-quality wines are sold by the bottle, but house wine is perfectly acceptable and it is priced by the litre so you can order as much or as little as you like.

Zagreb has its own brewery, producing Ožujsko lager and Tomislav dark beer, as well as foreign beers such as Stella Artois brewed under licence. Another good lager is Karlovačko, from the city of Karlovac. Mineral water, both still and sparkling, is available everywhere, along with bizarre combinations such as *bambus* (red wine and Cola) or *miš-maš* (red wine and orangeade).

If you feel like rounding off your meal with a digestif, choose from an array of *rakije*, fiery, grappa-like spirits. Popular varieties include *šljivovica* (plum brandy), *travarica* (herb brandy) and *biska* (mistletoe brandy), but it can also be made with blueberries, walnuts or figs.

USEFUL DINING PHRASES

I would like a table for ... people
Trebam stol za .... osoba
Tre-bam stol za ... 'o-so-ba

Waiter!/Waitress!
Konobar!/Konobarica!
Ko-no-bar!/Ko-no-ba-ri-tsa!

Can we have the bill, please?
Molim vas, možemo li dobiti račun?
Mo-lim vas, mo-zhe-mo li do-bi-ti ra-choon?

Could I have it well-cooked/medium/rare, please?
Molim vas, za mene dobro pečeno/polupečeno/
na engleski način?
*Mo-lim vas, za me-ne do-bro pe-che-no/'po-loo-pe-che-no/
na 'en-gle-ski na-chin?*

I am a vegetarian. Does this contain meat?
Ja sam vegetarijanac. Ima li ovo mesa?
Ya sam ve-ge-ta-ri-ya-nats. Ima li ovo me-sa?

Where is the toilet, please?
Molim vas, gdje je WC?
Mo-lim vas, gdie ye ve tse?

I would like a cup of/two cups of/another coffee/tea, please
Molim jednu/dvije/još jednu kavu/jedan/dva/još jedan čaj
*Mo-lim yed-noo/dvie/yosh yed-noo ka-voo/ye-dan/dva/
yosh ye-dan chay*

When the bill arrives, there will usually be a small cover charge for bread added on. Tipping is expected but does not need to be too heavy – 10 per cent or rounding up to the nearest 10 kn will do. Most restaurants accept credit cards nowadays, but it is a good idea to carry some cash just in case.

If you want to make up a picnic, the outdoor stalls at Dolac market sell fresh fruit and vegetables, and you can buy bread, cheese, ham and salami at the indoor market hall. There are also numerous *pekara* (bakeries), open from early morning to late at night, selling takeaway snacks like *burek* (filo pastry stuffed with minced meat or cottage cheese). For lunch on the go, street vendors sell corn on the cob in summer and roast chestnuts in winter, while fast-food outlets offer *ćevapčići* (little minced sausages), kebabs and pizza. Finally, there are few things the people of Zagreb enjoy more than sitting outside a café with a mountainous ice-cream sundae, piled high with lurid colours and flavours from pistachio to green apple, finished off with chocolate and whipped cream.

Entertainment & nightlife

Anyone who visited Zagreb in the 1980s or 1990s would not recognise the city's nightlife today. Independence and post-war freedom have given Zagreb a real buzz, with new jazz clubs, live music venues and fashionable lounge bars opening up every month.

For most people, a night out in summer means drinking at a terrace bar. A young crowd heads to Tkalčićeva to drink beer, while the nouveaux riches sip cocktails and champagne in the lounge bars of Bogovićeva or recline on sofas and cushions in the wine bars of Centar Kaptol.

Serious clubbers should head out to the shores of Lake Jarun for the hippest late-night vibes. Aquarius (see page 103) kick-started the Zagreb club scene when it opened in 1992 and it is still the place to beat, with occasional live bands and DJs playing hip-hop and electronica. The nearby Gallery is smarter and more sophisticated, with comfy sofas, funky sounds and a great lakeside terrace. For an edgier, more youthful scene, take the tram to Savski Most and wander along the north bank of the River Sava, where riverboats with names like *Brazil* and *Papillon* have been moored on the embankment and turned into late-night bars playing rock, urban, salsa, world music and Balkan turbo-folk beats.

Look out for posters advertising live gigs and club nights. The big pop and rock acts play at the **Dom Sportova sports hall** (ⓦ www.dom-sportova.hr) in the west of the city or at **Tvornica** (ⓦ www.tvornica-kulture.hr) near the bus station. Tickets are available from record shops such as Aquarius (see page 86)

and Dancing Bear (see page 87) or online from **Eventim**
(ⓦ www.eventim.hr). Jazz fans can catch live music most nights
at the renowned BP Club and Jazz Club (see page 92).

Cinemas show the latest international releases in their
original language with Croatian subtitles, which means that
most films are in (American) English. For the full state-of-the-art
experience, head for the multiplex cinemas inside the Centar
Kaptol and Branimirova shopping centres, which have wide
screens and comfortable seats. More traditional cinemas in the
city centre include **Europa** (ⓐ Varšavska 3), **Grič** (ⓐ Jurišićeva 6)
and **Zagreb** (ⓐ Trg Petra Preradovića 4).

Zagreb has a strong tradition of performing arts, including
drama, ballet, classical music and opera. Tickets for most events
are available on the door but they are cheaper if bought a day or
two in advance from the box office. At present, there is no central

🔺 *Something for everyone at popular Aquarius*

● *The hyper-hip Škola on Bogovićeva (see page 93)*

booking office for the city's concert halls and theatres. For more on music and drama, see Culture (see pages 20–2).

To find out what's on while you are in Zagreb, pick up a copy of *Events & Performances*, a monthly guide published by the city tourist board. Concerts and theatre performances are also listed in the local press and advertised on hoardings across the city. Another useful publication is *Zagreb In Your Pocket*, a savvy, pocket-sized magazine that comes out every two months and is available free from tourist offices and hotels; it has up-to-date listings of restaurants and bars and is particularly good at telling you what's hot on the local club scene. The free monthly guide *inZg* (Ⓦ www.inzg.net), available from the tourist office and online, is another good source of information on live music and club nights.

Sport & relaxation

SPECTATOR SPORTS

Sport is a huge source of national pride and triumphs such as victories in the Davis Cup tennis championship in 2005 and in the Olympic handball championship in 2004 unite the entire country in celebration. Sporting heroes include Goran Ivanišević, the 2001 Wimbledon men's singles tennis champion, and Janica Kostelić, the most successful female skier of all time.

Football is a national obsession. The Croatian team finished third at their first World Cup in 1998, turning captain Zvonimir Boban and striker Davor Šuker – winner of the Golden Boot award for the highest scorer – into instant celebrities. The national side play their matches at the **Maksimir Stadium** (🚇 Maksimirska Cesta 🚋 Tram: 4, 7, 11, 12 to Bukovačka), home of Dinamo Zagreb. Dinamo is one of the two biggest clubs in Croatia, along with rivals Hajduk Split. The stadium was expanded as part of Croatia's ultimately unsuccessful bid to host Euro 2012 and now holds

A LEGEND REMEMBERED

Dražen Petrović (1964–93) was the finest basketball player of his generation until his tragic death in a car crash at the age of 28. The home of Croatia's top team, Cibona, has been renamed **Dražen Petrović stadium** (🚇 Savska Cesta 30 🚋 Tram: 3, 9, 12 to Tehnički Muzej) in honour of their one-time player, while the nearby Cibona Tower houses the Dražen Petrović Memorial Museum.

60,000 spectators. The season runs from August to May. Tickets are on sale at kiosks outside the ground and can usually be bought cheaply on the day. League matches are also played at **NK Zagreb** (ⓐ Kranjčevićeva Ⓝ Tram: 3, 9, 12 to Badalićeva). Fixtures are published online in Croatian at ⓦ www.prva-hnl.hr

PARTICIPATION SPORTS

Medvednica (see page 99) is a giant outdoor playground, with enough hiking trails to keep you happy for days. In winter, you can even go skiing here (ⓦ www.sljeme-skijanje.com). In summer, head for Lake Jarun (see page 95) for swimming, canoeing, kayaking, windsurfing and tennis, or hire a bike to make a circuit of the lake. Golf is the fastest-growing sport in Croatia and Zagreb now has its own **Golf & Country Club** (ⓞ 01 653 1177 ⓦ www.gcc.zagreb.hr), with a 9-hole course beside the River Sava.

⬤ To the max: the Maksimir Stadium

Accommodation

Until recently, most accommodation in Zagreb was aimed firmly at business travellers and there was a shortage of budget options and mid-priced hotels. Thankfully, that is now changing, as low-cost flights open up Zagreb to a new generation of travellers. The major international brands like Sheraton and Westin have hotels in the city, offering all the 5-star luxury you would expect, but there is also a growing number of backpackers' hostels and small, family-run hotels.

Hotel prices are often quoted in euros, but you will be expected to pay in kuna. Credit cards are usually accepted, though there may be a discount for paying in cash. A single room is typically between 60 and 80 per cent of the cost of a double, and prices tend to rise by around 20 per cent during the Zagreb Trade Fair in September. In addition, all visitors must pay a tourist tax of around 7 kn per person per night. Most hotels, even at the lower price range, have air conditioning, central heating, satellite TV channels and internet access.

If you are staying in Zagreb for more than a few days, consider renting a self-catering apartment through **NEST** (❶ 01 487 3225 Ⓦ www.nest.hr) or **InZagreb** (❶ 01 652 3201 Ⓦ www.inzagreb.com).

PRICE CATEGORIES

The symbols indicate the average cost of a double room, including breakfast.

£ up to 600 kn   ££ 600–1,000 kn   £££ over 1,000 kn

Both agencies offer stylish city centre apartments with all mod cons including microwaves, CD and DVD players for less than the cost of a double room in a mid-priced hotel. Another option for budget travellers is to rent a room with a local family through **Evistas** (ⓐ Augusta Šenoe 28 ⓣ 01 483 9554 ⓔ evistas@zg.t-com.hr), which will not only save you money but also give you an insight into Croatian life.

HOTELS

Hotel Ilica £ This small, cosy hotel two tram stops from the main square offers a great combination of luxury and value. ⓐ Ilica 102 (Donji grad) ⓣ 01 377 7522 ⓦ www.hotel-ilica.hr ⓝ Tram: 1, 6, 11 to Britanski trg ⓘ Credit cards not accepted

Movie Hotel £ Located above a cinema-themed pub (see page 104), this has 20 comfy film-themed rooms. ⓐ Savska Cesta 141 (Outside the centre) ⓣ 01 600 3600 ⓦ www.themoviehotel.com ⓝ Tram: 4, 5, 14, 17 to Prisavlje

Sliško £ This friendly, family-run hotel near the bus station is conveniently situated for travellers arriving on the airport bus. ⓐ Bunićeva 7 (Donji grad) ⓣ 01 618 4777 ⓦ www.slisko.hr ⓝ Tram: 2, 5, 6, 7, 8 to Autobusni Kolodvor

Arcotel Allegra ££ Funky, Austrian-owned design hotel near the railway station, with a DVD player in every room. ⓐ Branimirova 29 (Donji grad) ⓣ 01 469 6000 ⓦ www.arcotel.cc/allegra ⓝ Tram: 2, 6, 8 to Branimirova

Best Western Astoria ££ Elegant 1930s hotel that's showing
no sign of age. ⓐ Petrinjska 71 (Donji grad) ⓣ 01 480 8900
ⓦ www.bestwestern.com ⓣ Tram: 2, 4, 6, 9, 13 to Glavni kolodvor

Garny ££ An unexpected treat in the shadow of the airport,
this family-run hotel is bright, colourful and tastefully decorated.
ⓐ Mikulčićeva 7A, Velika Gorica (Outside the centre) ⓣ 01 625 3600
ⓦ www.hotel-garny.hr

Jaegerhorn ££ Centrally located hotel in a 19th-century shopping
arcade with a lovely terrace restaurant. ⓐ Ilica 14 (Donji grad)
ⓣ 01 483 3877 ⓦ www.hotel-pansion-jaegerhorn.hr ⓣ Tram: 1,
6, 11, 12, 13, 14, 17 to Trg bana Jelačića

🔺 *Funky and fun: the Arcotel Allegra*

Tomislavov dom ££ Old-style mountain lodge at the summit of Sljeme, a short walk from the ski slopes. Facilities include an indoor pool and spa. ⓐ Sljemenska Cesta 24 (Outside the centre) ⓣ 01 456 0400 ⓦ www.hotel-tomislavovdom.com Ⓝ Tram: 15 to Mihaljevac, then bus directly to the hotel

Dubrovnik £££ This enjoys a fabulous location in a 1920s building with a modern glass annexe. ⓐ Gajeva 1 (Donji grad) ⓣ 01 486 3555 ⓦ www.hotel-dubrovnik.hr Ⓝ Tram: 1, 6, 11, 12, 13, 14, 17 to Trg bana Jelačića

Palace £££ Zagreb's oldest hotel oozes elegance and charm, with rooms in a 19th-century Viennese palace overlooking a pretty park. ⓐ Strossmayerov trg 10 (Donji grad) ⓣ 01 489 9600 ⓦ www.palace.hr Ⓝ Tram: 6, 13 to Zrinjevac

● *Experience art deco splendour at the Regent Esplanade*

Regent Esplanade £££ Everyone who is anyone has stayed at the Esplanade, built in 1925 for passengers arriving on the Orient Express. With richly decorated rooms, an art deco lobby and every conceivable luxury, this is a real indulgence. ⓐ Mihanovićeva 1 (Donji grad) ⓣ 01 456 6666 ⓦ www.theregentzagreb.com ⓝ Tram: 2, 4, 6, 9, 13 to Glavni kolodvor

HOSTELS

Buzz Backpackers £ Clean, comfortable, central hostel with eight-bed dorm, private room with balcony and Wi-Fi internet access. ⓐ Đorđićeva 24 (Donji grad) ⓣ 01 481 6748 ⓦ www.buzzbackpackers.com ⓝ Tram: 4, 8 to Klinika za Traumatologiju

Fulir £ This small, friendly hostel near the main square was opened in 2006 by two young Croatians concerned at the lack of budget accommodation in Zagreb. ⓐ Radićeva 3A (Gornji grad) ⓣ 01 483 0882 ⓦ www.fulir-hostel.com ⓝ Tram: 1, 6, 11, 12, 13, 14, 17 to Trg bana Jelačića

Nocturno £ Single, double and triple rooms above a restaurant in the heart of the action between Tkalčićeva and Dolac market. Open 24 hours. ⓐ Skalinska 2A (Gornji grad) ⓣ 01 481 3325 ⓦ www.nocturno.hr ⓝ Tram: 1, 6, 11, 12, 13, 14, 17 to Trg bana Jelačića

Ravnice Youth Hostel £ Highly recommended hostel close to Maksimir Park. ⓐ I Ravnice 38D (Outside the centre) ⓣ 01 233 2325 ⓦ www.ravnice-youth-hostel.hr ⓝ Tram: 4, 7, 11, 12 to Ravnice

THE BEST OF ZAGREB

There is a whole range of attractions for the visitor to Zagreb, but here are some of the sights and experiences you really shouldn't miss on any trip to the city.

TOP 10 ATTRACTIONS

- **Gornji grad** Take the funicular – a memorable experience in itself – to the oldest part of the city, which is a compact cornucopia of sightseeing delights (see page 66)

- **Tkalčićeva** Strut your stuff with the see and be seen brigade on Zagreb's prettiest promenade, which is a catwalk for the city's night-time glitterati (see page 65)

- **Trg bana Jelačića** Coffee and people-watching in this, the heart and soul of the city, is an essential Zagreb experience (see page 77)

- **Muzej grada Zagreba (Zagreb City Museum)** Discover 1,000 years of city history, including eye-popping footage of more recent upheavals (see page 69)

⬇ *The city from the Kula Lotrščak*

- **Arheološki muzej (Archaeological Museum)** See the Vučedol Dove, Croatia's oldest work of art and a poignant symbol of its age-old yearning for peace, alongside many other fascinating exhibits (see page 82)

- **Hrvatsko narodno kazalište (Croatian National Theatre)** The city's go-to location for high-cultural performances is an architectural treat, built as it was in the tradition of the great European opera houses (see page 93)

- **Maksimir Park** A venerable playground for all ages that's crammed full of delights and is a great place for a stroll (see page 98)

- **Mirogoj Cemetery** An eloquently moving tribute to the city's dead, including paupers and princes and victims of the recent war (see page 100)

- **Medvednica** If your batteries need recharging, leave the city behind by donning those walking boots and heading for the hills (see page 99)

- **Samobor** Sample sausage, custard tarts and riverside walks in this perfect, pastel-pretty provincial town (see page 106)

RUKOTVORINE

Suggested itineraries

HALF-DAY: ZAGREB IN A HURRY

If you only have a short time to spare, take the funicular to Gornji grad to explore the oldest part of the city and admire the coloured roof tiles of St Mark's Church. If you have time, you may like to pop into the Croatian Naïve Art Museum (see page 68) or Ivan Meštrović Foundation (see page 68) to see some modern art. Leave by the Kamenita vrata (Stone Gate) and cross Krvavi Most (Bloody Bridge) to Tkalčićeva to stroll along Zagreb's favourite promenade. Return along Kaptol and have a quick look around the cathedral (see page 61) before finishing with a coffee on Trg bana Jelačića.

1 DAY: TIME TO SEE A LITTLE MORE

If you have a full day, you should also have time to see something of Donji grad. It takes about an hour to walk the 'Green Horseshoe' from Trg bana Jelačića to the railway station, through the Botanical Garden (see page 76) and back via the Croatian National Theatre (see page 93). Along the way, you pass the city's major museums, so stop off and visit one of them if you have time. Alternatively, treat yourself to a special lunch at Paviljon (see page 92).

2–3 DAYS: TIME TO SEE MUCH MORE

Over a long weekend, you can easily do all of the above and also explore beyond the city centre. If the weather is good, buy picnic food from Dolac market and hop on a tram to Maksimir Park (see page 98) or take the children to see the zoo. You could even spend a full day on Medvednica (see page 99) – take the bus up and walk back down, enjoying the views on the way.

LONGER: ENJOYING ZAGREB TO THE FULL

With four or more days, you can really get to know Zagreb and its surroundings. Be sure to spend at least one day out of the city, visiting the attractive town of Samobor (see page 106) or the baroque former capital at Varaždin (see page 116).

◔ The winding streets of historic Zagreb

Something for nothing

Zagreb's favourite pastime is also one of the cheapest – observing the world from a seat at a pavement café. Take a book or a newspaper, order a coffee, write your postcards or just indulge in that old-fashioned sport of people-watching. Your coffee will come with a glass of water and nobody will complain if you make it last two hours.

Afterwards, you could go for a stroll in one of the city parks. Maksimir (see page 98) is the grandfather of all Zagreb parks, but Ribnjak (see page 64) and Zrinjevac (see page 81) are good choices in the city centre. In summer, you might stumble across an open-air concert or an impromptu performance from a busker. Don't miss the free promenade concerts in the bandstand at Zrinjevac, which take place on Saturday mornings (11.00–13.00)

THE ZAGREB CARD

The Zagreb Card isn't free but it can certainly save you money if you are spending a few days in Zagreb. Available at tourist offices, the airport arrivals hall, bus station, railway station and hotels, it costs 90 kn for 72 hours. The benefits include unlimited public transport on buses, trams, the Gradec funicular and Medvednica bus, half-price entry at museums and discounts at cinemas, theatres, concert halls, restaurants, bars and shops. The card must be signed and you must fill in the date and time the first time that you use it.

⬥ *The belvedere in Maksimir Park*

from May to September and feature everything from big bands to mariachi, together with children's entertainment and actors in 19th-century period costume.

None of Zagreb's museums is expensive to visit, but there is free entry at the Croatian History Museum (see page 68) on Mondays and the Ethnographic Museum (see page 83) on Thursdays, while the Zagreb City Museum (see page 69) offers free guided tours at 11.00 on Saturday and Sunday. Children under seven are normally admitted free to museums, while kids from seven to fifteen pay half-price.

When it rains

Zagreb's museums provide the perfect solution to the problem of what to do on a rainy day. Although few of them contain world-class exhibits or works of art, you can easily while away a few hours waiting for the weather to improve.

If the grey skies are getting you down, head for the museum triangle on the west side of Trg maršala Tita, where three of Zagreb's most august institutions are found almost side by side. Biggest of the lot is the Mimara Museum (see page 84), with an eclectic collection ranging from Egyptian glassware to French Impressionists. The nearby Arts & Crafts Museum (see page 85) has furniture, paintings and pottery spanning several centuries, and also puts on imaginative temporary exhibitions. Take your time browsing in the museum shop, which sells glassware and jewellery by contemporary Croatian designers. Finally, the Ethnographic Museum (see page 83) features Croatian folk costumes and an Aladdin's Cave of objects brought back by Croatian explorers from their travels.

If you need a break from all that museum-bashing, Kavana Kazalište (usually known as Kavkaz) is a lovely Viennese-style coffee house across the square, with soft leather chairs and a long literary and theatrical history. For lunch, Hrvatski kulturni klub (see page 90) in the basement of the Arts & Crafts Museum serves first-class Croatian food.

Alternatively, you could always go shopping. If you don't want to get wet traipsing along Ilica, head for Centar Kaptol, a modern indoor shopping mall with three floors of trendy bars and boutiques near the cathedral. There is even a cinema on the top floor, where you can catch the latest Hollywood movies in English, while falling asleep in a comfortable seat with its own headrest. Believe it or not, one of the biggest shops at Centar Kaptol is a branch of the British clothing chain Marks & Spencer. If all else fails, buy yourself an umbrella and head back out into the rain.

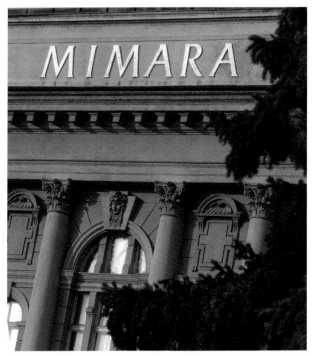

⬧ *Marvel at the Mimara*

On arrival

TIME DIFFERENCE
Croatia is on Central European Time (CET), which is an hour ahead of Greenwich Mean Time (GMT). Daylight Saving applies: clocks are put forward one hour at the end of March and back one hour at the end of October.

ARRIVING
By air
Zagreb's Pleso airport (international code ZAG) is situated 16 km (10 miles) south of the city. There are banks and ATMs in the arrivals hall. The easiest way of getting into town is on the Croatia Airlines shuttle bus, which leaves every 30 minutes from 07.00–20.00, with later departures timed to follow flight arrivals. The journey takes less than 30 minutes and a ticket costs 30 kn. The bus arrives at the Croatia Airlines terminal, next to the main bus station.

A taxi from the airport will cost around 200–250 kn to Zagreb city centre.

By rail
International and long-distance trains arrive at the Glavni kolodvor (railway station), 1 km (½ mile) south of Trg bana Jelačića. Cross the road in front of the station and keep walking past the statue of King Tomislav, or take tram 6 or 13 for two stops to arrive at the main square.

By road

International and long-distance buses arrive at the Autobusni kolodvor (bus station), 1.5 km (1 mile) southwest of the city centre. Tram 6 departs from outside the bus station, taking five stops to reach Trg bana Jelačića.

FINDING YOUR FEET

Zagreb is an easy city to get around. Crime is not a major problem, but petty theft can occur, and newly arrived tourists make for easy prey. Keep your wallet and valuables securely hidden, and keep an eye out for pickpockets on crowded trams.

⬤ *Keep your eye on the clock at the railway station*

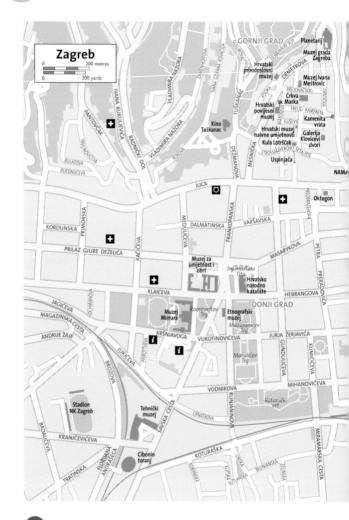

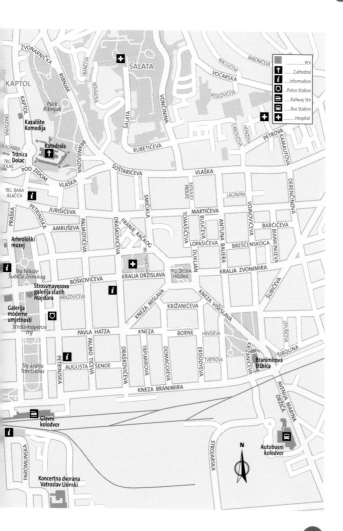

ORIENTATION

Zagreb lies between the wooded slopes of Medvednica to the north and the River Sava to the south. Most sights of interest are found in a relatively small area around the main square, Trg bana Jelačića, with Gornji grad (Upper town) to the north and Donji grad (Lower town) to the south. The tourist office is situated on Trg bana Jelačića. Gornji grad is compact and easily explored on foot, while Donji grad is slightly more spread out and you may need to use the trams.

GETTING AROUND

Zagreb has an efficient public transport network, operated by ZET (Zagreb Electric Tram Company). The city centre is served by trams, while buses link the city to the suburbs. Many bus routes begin at the end of tram lines, making it easy to switch from one to the other.

MAKING SENSE OF STREET NAMES

You may well be confused by the apparent discrepancy between the names on the map and those used in street signs and in addresses. In part, this is a result of Croatian grammar, which changes word endings according to the meaning, and in part a matter of convention. Thus, ulica Ljudevita Gaja is commonly known as Gajeva, ulica Nikole Tesle is known as Teslina, ulica Ivana Tkalčića becomes Tkalčićeva and ulica Ivana Gundulića turns into Gundulićeva. The same applies to squares, with Trg maršala Tita becoming Titov Trg and Trg bana Jelačića also known as Jelačićev Trg.

IF YOU GET LOST, TRY ...

Excuse me, do you speak English?
Oprostite, govorite li engleski?
O-'pro-sti-te, 'go-vo-ri-te li 'en-gle-ski?

Can you tell me the way to the bus station/taxi rank/ city centre?
Možete li mi reći kako mogu doći do autobusnog kolodvora/taksi-stajališta/centra grada?
'Mo-zhe-te li mi re-chi ka-ko mo-goo do-chi do 'a-oo-toboos-nog 'ko-lo-dvo-ra/tak-si 'sta-ya-li-shta/tsen-tra gra-da?

Can you point to it on my map?
Možete li mi to pokazati na planu grada?
'Mo-zhe-te li mi to po-'ka-za-ti na pla-noo gra-da?

Trams on most routes run every few minutes from 04.00–00.00, with a reduced service at night. A map of the network is displayed at most stops and trams are marked with their route number and final destination. A ticket for Zone 1 covers all of the sights in this book (except Samobor and Varaždin) and is valid on buses and trams for 90 minutes; it includes changes. A single ticket costs 8 kn in advance from newspaper kiosks and 10 kn from the driver. Night fares (from midnight to 04.00) are double. A one-day pass for buses and trams costs 25 kn. You must show your ticket to the driver (on buses) or punch it in

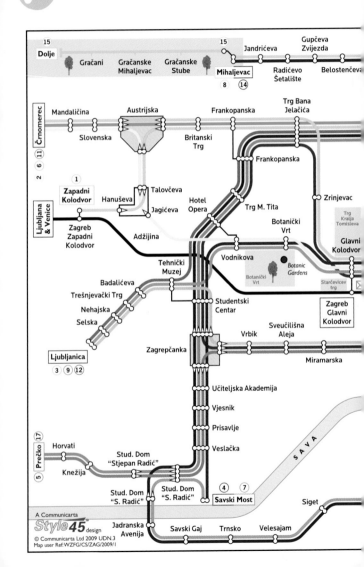

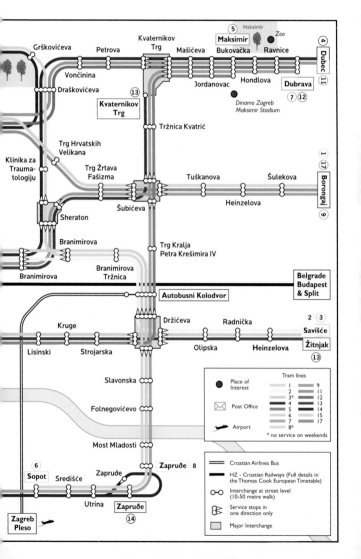

the on-board machine (on trams). Children under six years old travel free. The Zagreb Card (see page 46) gives free travel for 72 hours on buses and trams as well as the Gradec funicular and Medvednica bus. For journeys outside the city, buy a ticket from the main bus station.

Taxis are readily available at the bus and railway stations and major hotels, and there are taxi ranks near the cathedral and Croatian National Theatre. You can also call a radio taxi by telephone on ❶ 970. Make sure that the meter is switched on before you set off. Taxi drivers expect a tip, but rounding the fare up to the nearest 10 kn should be enough.

CAR HIRE

Driving a car in Zagreb is not for the faint-hearted, and public transport is reliable. If you do want to hire a car to explore more independently, however, the following companies have offices in the city centre and at the airport. The best rates are generally available if you book online in advance.

Avis ❶ 062 222 226 Ⓦ www.avis.com.hr

Budget ❶ 01 480 5688 Ⓦ www.budget.hr

Europcar ❶ 01 483 6045 Ⓦ www.europcar.hr

Hertz ❶ 062 727 277 Ⓦ www.hertz.hr

National ❶ 021 399 043 Ⓦ www.nationalcar.hr

❶ *Statues and spires: Kaptol*

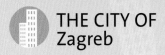

Gornji grad (Upper town)

Gornji grad is where it all began. The twin towns of Gradec and
Kaptol grew up side by side beneath the mountain of Medvednica.
Gradec, a so-called 'free royal city' by royal decree since 1242, was
fortified, with walls and towers whose remnants can still be seen
today, to protect it from invading Turks and Mongols. The two
were divided by the Medveščak brook, which flowed where
Tkalčićeva is today. Occasionally, disputes between Gradec and
Kaptol would turn into outright battles, hence the name Krvavi
Most (Bloody Bridge) for the short street linking Radićeva to
Tkalčićeva. Even now, there is continuing rivalry between Gradec
and Kaptol, the centres of political and religious power. For
centuries, Gradec has been the seat of the Croatian government
while Kaptol has been the seat of the Catholic Church. You cannot
fail to notice that Gradec is full of policemen guarding the
Parliament and presidential palace, while Kaptol seems to be
largely populated by priests, nuns and religious bookshops.

Today, Gradec is one of the most attractive areas of the city,
with 19th-century houses, leafy lanes, cobbled streets, art galleries
and museums. All of the sights are within walking distance of
each other and the only way to get around is on foot – though
if you don't want to traipse up the hill to get there, you can save
your legs by hitching a ride on a charming funicular railway.

SIGHTS & ATTRACTIONS

Kamenita vrata (Stone Gate)

The Stone Gate is the only survivor of the four original entrance gates to Gradec. Its present appearance dates from 1760, when it was rebuilt after a fire. According to legend, a painting of the Virgin Mary was found unharmed in the ashes and it has now been turned into a shrine. The image is kept behind a beautiful baroque grille and attracts numerous pilgrims who can be seen praying and lighting candles at all hours of the day. If you want to join them, nuns sell candles from a kiosk inside the gate. This place is a moving testament to the enduring strength of the Catholic Church in Croatia. ⓐ North of Trg bana Jelačića Ⓝ Tram: 1, 6, 11, 12, 13, 14, 17 to Trg bana Jelačića

Katedrala (Cathedral)

The twin spires of Zagreb's cathedral dominate the upper town. The first church was built here in the 12th century, but the cathedral you see today was designed by Hermann Bollé, the architect who played a key role in rebuilding Zagreb after the 1880 earthquake. Inside, crowds flock to the tomb of Cardinal Alojzije Stepinac (1898–1960), a former archbishop of Zagreb who was imprisoned under the Communist regime. In front of the cathedral, the gleaming golden statues of the Virgin Mary and angels are the work of Viennese sculptor Anton Fernkorn, who also designed the statue of Josip Jelačić in Trg bana Jelačića. ⓐ Kaptol ⓣ 01 481 4727 ⓗ 08.00–20.00 Ⓝ Tram: 1, 6, 11, 12, 13, 14, 17 to Trg bana Jelačića

Kula Lotrščak (Lotrščak Tower)

This tall square tower, part of the original 13th-century fortifications of Gradec, is the first thing you see when you emerge from the upper funicular terminus. Try to time your visit to arrive at 12.00,

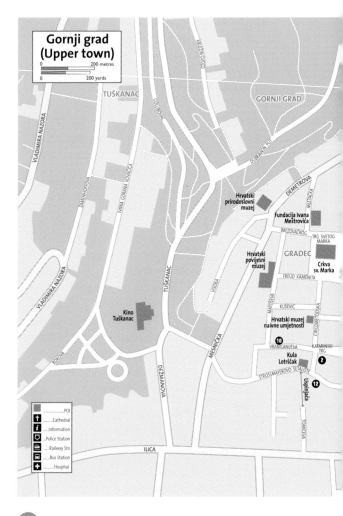

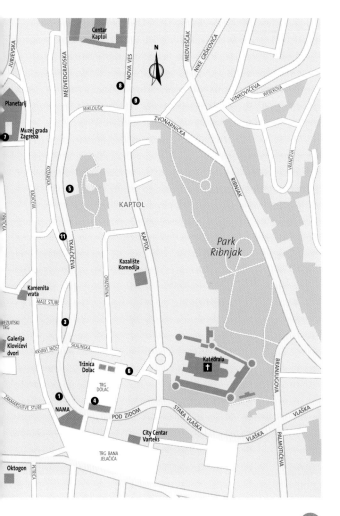

when a noon cannon is fired from the tower in a tradition dating back to 1877. You can watch the spectacle from below, or go inside the tower to see the cannoneer in his distinctive blue military uniform. Afterwards, climb the spiral staircase for views from the rooftop. ⓐ Strossmayerovo šetalište 9 ⓣ 01 485 1768 ⓛ 11.00–19.00 ⓝ Tram: 1, 6, 11, 12, 13, 14, 17 to Trg bana Jelačića, then funicular up Tomićeva. Admission charge

Ribnjak

This peaceful park in the shadow of the cathedral takes its name from the fishponds that used to supply the bishop's table. With shady paths and benches, it makes a good place to relax on a summer day, enjoying views of the cathedral, Archbishop's

● *The firing of the cannon at Kula Lotrščak*

THE WITCH FROM GRIČ

As you wander along Tkalčićeva, you may notice a bronze statue of a woman with an umbrella keeping an eye on the passers-by. This is Marija Jurić Zagorka (1873–1957), the first female journalist in Croatia and the author of popular stories set in Zagreb including *Grička Vještica* (*The Witch from Grič*).

Palace and the eastern walls of Kaptol. Ⓝ Tram: 4, 8, 11, 12, 14 to Draškovićeva

Strossmayerovo šetalište

This leafy promenade, named after Bishop Strossmayer (see page 85), follows the course of the former defensive wall of Gradec. Today, it offers fine views over the city, especially at its eastern end, where a terrace overlooks the cathedral and the onion-domed spire of St Mary's Church.

Tkalčićeva

You haven't really seen Zagreb until you have spent an evening on Tkalčićeva, admiring the city's young and beautiful as they strut their stuff during the *korzo*. This pretty street of 19th-century houses with wooden balconies and pastel façades was built on the site of the dried-up stream that once divided Gradec from Kaptol. Today, the street has become Zagreb's favourite promenade, at its liveliest on warm summer nights. Ⓝ Tram: 1, 6, 11, 12, 13, 14, 17 to Trg bana Jelačića

ON THE TILES

The mosaic roof tiles of St Mark's Church were added in the 19th century to symbolise the unification of the three separate provinces of Croatia. The left-hand shield features the red-and-white chequerboard of Croatia, the three lions of Dalmatia and the pine marten of Slavonia, seen running between the rivers Drava and Sava. The right-hand shield features the historic coat of arms of Zagreb: a castle with three towers beneath a crescent moon and star.

Trg svetog Marka (St Mark's Square)

The main square at the heart of Gradec is surrounded by the great institutions of state. On one side is Banski Dvori, the 19th-century governor's palace now housing the office of the Croatian president; on the other is the Sabor (Parliament), where independence from Yugoslavia was declared in 1991. At the centre of the square, **Crkva sv. Marka** (St Mark's Church, ◷ 07.00–20.00) is the oldest parish church in Zagreb, built in the 13th century. Inside, you will find a Crucifixion and Madonna by Ivan Meštrović (see page 68), but the most notable feature is the roof with its coloured mosaic tiles depicting the coats of arms of Croatia and Zagreb. Ⓝ Tram: 1, 6, 11, 12, 13, 14, 17 to Trg bana Jelačića, then funicular up Tomićeva, or walk

Uspinjača (Funicular)

The easiest and most enjoyable way of getting to Gornji grad is on the funicular railway, which opened in 1890 and is popularly known as the 'old lady of Zagreb'. The single carriage seats 16 passengers and makes the short ascent from Tomićeva in just 55 seconds. There is a flight of steps running alongside the rails, but the gradient is steep and the journey is such fun that everyone should do it at least once. ● Every ten minutes from 06.30–21.00 Ⓝ Tram: 1, 6, 11, 12, 13, 14, 17 to Trg bana Jelačića

▲ The 'old lady of Zagreb' will get you up the hill

CULTURE

Fundacija Ivana Meštrovića (Ivan Meštrović Foundation)

This museum occupies the former home and studio of Ivan Meštrović (1883–1962), who was known as 'the Croatian Rodin' for his sensual and expressive sculptures. More than 100 of his works are on display. ⓐ Mletačka 8 ⓣ 01 485 1123 ⓦ www.mdc.hr/mestrovic ⓛ 10.00–18.00 Tues–Fri, 10.00–14.00 Sat & Sun ⓝ Tram: 1, 6, 11, 12, 13, 14, 17 to Trg bana Jelačića. Admission charge

Galerija Klovićevi dvori (Klovićevi Dvori Gallery)

A former Jesuit monastery has been converted into a stunning art gallery with a changing programme of exhibitions. While you are here, check out St Catherine's Church, a 17th-century baroque masterpiece on the same square with a glistening white façade and a riot of pink stucco on the walls. ⓐ Jezuitski Trg 4 ⓣ 01 485 1926 ⓦ www.galerijaklovic.hr ⓛ 10.00–20.00 Tues–Sun ⓝ Tram: 1, 6, 11, 12, 13, 14, 17 to Trg bana Jelačića. Admission charge

Hrvatski muzej naivne umjetnosti (Croatian Naïve Art Museum)

This small museum near the Lotrščak Tower is dedicated to the tradition of naïve art in Croatia, which began in the 1930s in the village of Hlebine. This is a charming museum that you can visit in under an hour. ⓐ Ćirilometodska 3 ⓣ 01 485 1911 ⓦ www.hmnu.org ⓛ 10.00–18.00 Tues–Fri, 10.00–13.00 Sat & Sun. Admission charge

Hrvatski povijesni muzej (Croatian History Museum)

Housed in an 18th-century palace complete with ballroom and grand staircase, this museum provides a glimpse into the lifestyle of the Habsburg aristocracy in Zagreb. The collection is shown in a series of themed historical exhibitions. ⓐ Matoševa 9 ⓕ 01 485 1900 ⓦ www.hismus.hr ⓛ 10.00–18.00 Mon–Fri, 10.00–13.00 Sat & Sun ⓝ Tram: 1, 6, 11, 12, 13, 14, 17 to Trg bana Jelačića. Admission charge

Hrvatski prirodoslovni muzej (Croatian Natural History Museum)

Strictly one for the children or to kill time on a rainy day, this museum contains old-style display cases filled with stuffed animals, birds, fossils, rocks and shells. ⓐ Demetrova 1 ⓕ 01 485 1700 ⓦ www.hpm.hr ⓛ 10.00–17.00 Tues, Wed & Fri, 10.00–22.00 Thur, 10.00–19.00 Sat, 10.00–13.00 Sun ⓝ Tram: 1, 6, 11, 12, 13, 14, 17 to Trg bana Jelačića. Admission charge

Muzej grada Zagreba (Zagreb City Museum)

The story of Zagreb comes to life at this fascinating museum, which provides an enjoyable jaunt through 1,000 years of city history with the help of artefacts, scale models and imaginative displays. Don't miss the display of broken furniture and crockery

STARGAZING

The medieval Popov Toranj (Priests' Tower), beside the City Museum, has been home to Zagreb's planetarium (*planetarij*) and astronomical observatory since 1903. On clear evenings, you can climb onto the roof to gaze at the stars and planets through a powerful telescope, housed inside a specially built dome. ⓐ Opatička 22 ⓕ 01 485 1355 ⓛ 20.00–22.00 Tues–Fri. Admission charge from the rocket attack on the presidential palace in 1991, complete with video footage of the attack. Opatička 20 01 485 1364 www.mdc.hr/mgz 10.00–18.00 Tues, Wed & Fri, 10.00–22.00 Thur, 11.00–19.00 Sat, 10.00–14.00 Sun Tram: 1, 6, 11, 12, 13, 14, 17 to Trg bana Jelačića. Admission charge

RETAIL THERAPY

The high-street fashion brands are found at Centar Kaptol. For a selection of quirky, one-of-a-kind boutiques, head for Radićeva and Tkalčićeva.

Arkadija This gallery sells unusual gifts such as carnival masks and ceremonial swords. The neighbouring Bil-Ani specialises in miniature models of Croatian buildings. Radićeva 35 01 492 0704 09.00–20.00 Mon–Sat, 10.00–17.00 Sun Tram: 1, 6, 11, 12, 13, 14, 17 to Trg bana Jelačića

Aromatica Natural soaps, shampoos and massage oils from Adriatic plants, sold in attractively packaged gift boxes. Vlaška 7 01 481 1584 www.aromatica.hr 08.00–20.00 Mon–Fri, 08.00–15.00 Sat Tram: 4, 8, 11, 12, 14 to Draškovićeva

Centar Kaptol This three-storey shopping mall has a wide range of clothes and jewellery shops, cafés, bars and a cinema. The main entrance is on Nova ves but there is another entrance on Medvedgradska, an extension of Tkalčićeva. Nova ves 17 01 486 0241 09.00–21.00 Mon–Sat Tram: 1, 6, 11, 12, 13, 14, 17 to Trg bana Jelačića

Lazer Rok Jewellery is turned into sc[...]
boutique, where cutting-edge jeweller[...]
and expensive designs from an open-[...]
☎ 01 481 4030 🕒 10.00–20.00 Mon–Fr[...]
Ⓝ Tram: 1, 6, 11, 12, 13, 14, 17 to Trg bana [...]

Natura Croatica Croatian wines, spirits, olive oil and honey are
on sale at this small shop near the cathedral. ⓐ Pod Zidom 5
☎ 01 485 5076 🕒 09.00–21.00 Mon–Fri, 10.00–16.00 Sat
Ⓝ Tram: 1, 6, 11, 12, 13, 14, 17 to Trg bana Jelačića

Tržnica Dolac Zagreb's biggest market takes place each morning
on a raised terrace above Trg bana Jelačića. This is a feast for all
the senses, with farmers from the nearby countryside selling fruit,
vegetables, eggs and cheese. Beneath the square, an indoor market
hall has deli counters. There is also a fish market in a separate
building on the west side of the square. ⓐ Trg Dolac 🕒 06.00–14.00
Mon–Sat, 06.00–12.00 Sun Ⓝ Tram: 1, 6, 11, 12, 13, 14, 17 to
Trg bana Jelačića

Vinoteka Bornstein Zagreb's top wine shop is found in a brick-vaulted
cellar near the cathedral. It stocks a wide variety of Croatian wines,
spirits and liqueurs plus gastronomic treats like truffles and olive oil.
ⓐ Kaptol 19 ☎ 01 481 2361 ⓦ www.bornstein.hr 🕒 09.00–20.00
Mon–Sat Ⓝ Tram: 1, 6, 11, 12, 13, 14, 17 to Trg bana Jelačića

TAKING A BREAK

100% Liquid Health £ ❶ If you can't take any more coffee,

...eline for this juice bar, which has a great selection
...oothies, yoghurt drinks and freshly squeezed fruit juices.
...kalčićeva 5  01 482 8886 10.30–22.00 Mon–Sat
Tram: 1, 6, 11, 12, 13, 14, 17 to Trg bana Jelačića

Gornji grad £ ❷ This café with outdoor tables on a pretty square
in Gradec serves a simple menu of sandwiches, pizzas and snacks.
Katarininski Trg 01 485 1775 09.00–00.00 Tram: 1, 6, 11,
12, 13, 14, 17 to Trg bana Jelačića

Mangiare £ ❸ Thin-crust pizzas cooked the Italian way in a
proper brick oven, plus great salads and desserts. Tkalčićeva 29
01 482 8173 09.00–23.00 Mon–Sat, 12.00–23.00 Sun
Tram: 1, 6, 11, 12, 13, 14, 17 to Trg bana Jelačića

Rubelj Grill £ ❹ Situated on a terrace beneath Dolac market, this
is a good place for an inexpensive lunchtime snack of *ćevapčići*
served in a crusty bread bap. Trg Dolac 2 01 481 8777
09.00–23.00 Tram: 1, 6, 11, 12, 13, 14, 17 to Trg bana Jelačića

Ivica i Marica, one of the finest restaurants in Zagreb

Ivica i Marica ££ ⑤ Healthy vegetarian and organic cuisine, including some meat and fish dishes, served by waiters in folk costume in a Hansel-and-Gretel cottage atmosphere (Ivica i Marica means Hansel and Gretel in Croatian). ⓐ Tkalčićeva 70 ❶ 01 481 7321 🕒 10.00–23.00 Mon–Fri (until 22.00 in winter), 09.00–23.00 Sat, 13.00–21.30 Sun Ⓝ Tram: 1, 6, 11, 12, 13, 14, 17 to Trg bana Jelačića

Kerempuh ££ ⑥ This busy restaurant changes its menu every day. The emphasis is on hearty Croatian comfort food. Lunch only, but informal snacks all day. ⓐ Kaptol 3 ❶ 01 481 9000 🕒 07.00–23.00 Mon–Sat, 07.30–16.00 Sun Ⓝ Tram: 1, 6, 11, 12, 13, 14, 17 to Trg bana Jelačića

Stara Vura ££ ⑦ If you feel like a break from the City Museum, this restaurant in a vaulted cellar in the basement serves classic Croatian meat and fish dishes. ⓐ Opatička 20 ❶ 01 485 1368 🕒 12.00–00.00 Mon–Sat Ⓝ Tram: 1, 6, 11, 12, 13, 14, 17 to Trg bana Jelačića

AFTER DARK

RESTAURANTS

Dizmus ££ ⑧ Go down the steps to this cellar bistro, which has a daily changing menu of good-value market specials. ⓐ Nova ves 5 ❶ 01 466 7072 🕒 12.00–23.00 Ⓝ Tram: 1, 6, 11, 12, 13, 14, 17 to Trg bana Jelačića

Baltazar £££ ⑨ This temple to grilled meat, in a courtyard at the top end of Kaptol, is popular with Zagreb's movers and shakers. The house special is steak topped with bacon wrapped around chicken liver, but there are cheaper options like sausages, *ćevapčići* and mixed grill. There is also a fish restaurant, Gašpar. ⓐ Nova ves 4 ⓣ 01 466 6999 ⓛ 12.00–00.00 Mon–Sat ⓝ Tram: 1, 6, 11, 12, 13, 14, 17 to Trg bana Jelačića

Fran's Reef £££ ❿ Opened in 2006 in a small house in Gradec, this restaurant serves superb steaks and funky French-Brazilian fusion cuisine – how about lobster with blackcurrant and coconut milk? Booking recommended. ⓐ Vranicanijeva 6 ⓣ 01 485 1287 ⓛ 09.00–00.00 Tues–Sun ⓝ Tram: 1, 6, 11, 12, 13, 14, 17 to Trg bana Jelačića

Panino £££ ⓫ An upmarket Italian restaurant, offering a creative menu of pasta and risotto dishes. ⓐ Tkalčićeva 43 ⓣ 01 481 3349 ⓛ 12.00–23.00 ⓝ Tram: 1, 6, 11, 12, 13, 14, 17 to Trg bana Jelačića

Pod gričkim topom £££ ⓬ Perfectly grilled fish and steak on a charming summer terrace, overlooking the city beneath the Lotrščak Tower. ⓐ Zakmardijeve Stube 5 ⓣ 01 483 3607 ⓛ 11.00–00.00 Mon–Sat ⓝ Tram: 1, 6, 11, 12, 13, 14, 17 to Trg bana Jelačića

BARS & CLUBS

Tkalčićeva is prime bar-hopping territory, with something to suit everyone. For a more sophisticated scene, go to Centar Kaptol, with its chic cocktail, wine and cigar bars.

Cica This great little *grapperia* (brandy bar) at the start of the Tkalčićeva strip has a wonderful array of spirits. ⓐ Tkalčićeva 8 ⓛ 09.00–00.00 ⓝ Tram: 1, 6, 11, 12, 13, 14, 17 to Trg bana Jelačića

Khala This trendy wine bar on the ground floor of Centar Kaptol has sofas, cushions, candles and a laid-back oriental vibe. ⓐ Nova ves 17 (entrance on Medvedgradska) ⓣ 01 466 7140 ⓛ 08.00–01.00 Mon–Thur, 08.00–03.00 Fri & Sat, 09.00–01.00 Sun ⓝ Tram: 1, 6, 11, 12, 13, 14, 17 to Trg bana Jelačića

CINEMAS

Broadway Tkalča This five-screen multiplex on the top floor of Centar Kaptol shows the latest Hollywood and international releases. ⓐ Nova ves 17 ⓣ 01 486 0241 ⓦ www.broadway-kina.com ⓝ Tram: 1, 6, 11, 12, 13, 14, 17 to Trg bana Jelačića

Kino Tuškanac Zagreb's arthouse cinema shows Croatian and foreign films. The third weekend of every month is devoted to Queer Friday and Saturday for Zagreb's gay community. ⓐ Tuškanac 1 ⓣ 01 484 8771 ⓦ www.filmski-programi.hr ⓝ Tram: 2, 6, 11 to Frankopanska

THEATRES

Kazalište Komedija This small theatre near the cathedral stages musicals, operettas and plays in Croatian. ⓐ Kaptol 9 ⓣ 01 481 3200 ⓦ www.komedija.hr ⓛ Tickets go on sale one hour before performance; advance box office at Oktogon, Ilica 5 ⓝ Tram: 1, 6, 11, 12, 13, 14, 17 to Trg bana Jelačića

Kazalište Mala scena (Small Stage Theatre) Home to the English Language Theatre of Zagreb. ⓐ Medveščak 2 ⓣ 01 468 3352 ⓦ www.mala-scena.hr ⓝ Tram: 8, 14 to Grškovićeva

Donji grad (Lower town)

By the mid-19th century, Zagreb had grown beyond the boundaries of Gradec and Kaptol and needed to expand south towards the River Sava. The result was Donji grad, an early example of town planning designed using a Manhattan-style grid plan of intersecting avenues. At its heart was the Zelena potkova (Green Horseshoe), conceived by the architect Milan Lenuci as a continuous series of promenades and gardens, where the wealthy citizens of Zagreb could spend their leisure time. As well as parks, the Green Horseshoe was to contain the city's leading cultural and educational institutions, including museums, theatres, libraries and Zagreb University. Although it was never completed, you can still make out the U-shaped pattern of the Green Horseshoe on maps of Donji grad, stretching south from Trg maršala Tita to the Botanical Garden and north from the railway station to Trg Nikole Šubića Zrinskog (Zrinjevac Park). The best way to get the feel of this area is to walk around the Green Horseshoe, admiring the fine examples of Habsburg architecture along the way.

SIGHTS & ATTRACTIONS

Botanički vrt (Botanical Garden)

The centrepiece of the Green Horseshoe is this English-style landscaped garden, laid out in 1890. With bridges, ponds and avenues of trees, including sequoia, cypress, magnolia and pine, it makes a pleasant place for a stroll. At the heart of the garden is a floral parterre with rose beds, lawns and fountains, similar to those found in the grand palaces of France. From here you have a good view of the former University Library, now the Croatian State Archive, housed in a magnificent art nouveau building with bronze owls on the roof. ➋ Marulićev trg 9 ☎ 01 484 4002 🌐 http://hirc.botanic.hr/vrt/home.htm 🕐 09.00–14.30 Mon & Tues, 09.00–18.00 Wed–Sun, Apr–Oct ⊘ Tram: 2, 4, 9 to Botanički vrt

Trg bana Jelačića (Josip Jelačića Square)

With clanking trams, newspaper kiosks and 19th-century architecture, Trg bana Jelačića is the heartbeat of Zagreb and there is no better way to take the pulse of the city than from a seat at one of its pavement cafés. You cannot spend long in Zagreb before arriving at this square and the clock at its western end and fountain at its eastern end make natural meeting places during the evening *korzo*. Between the two is a large equestrian statue of Josip Jelačić, the nationalist hero after whom the square is named. During the Tito era, the statue was dismantled and

WHO WAS JOSIP JELAČIĆ?

Josip Jelačić (1801–59) is a Croatian icon. Appointed *ban* (governor) of Croatia by the Austrian emperor in 1848, he quickly allied himself with the ideals of the Croatian National Revival, a political and cultural movement that promoted a renaissance of Croatian language and literature. As governor, he abolished slavery, waged war on Hungary and united the provinces of Croatia, Slavonia and Dalmatia into a single nation, thus laying the foundations for the modern state of Croatia.

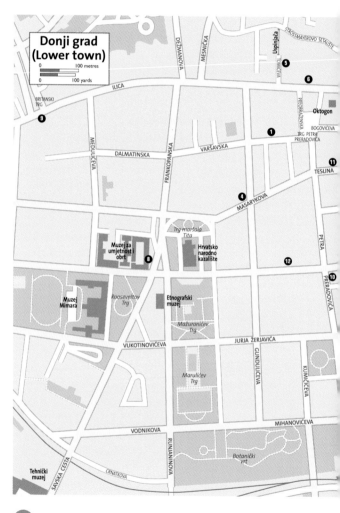

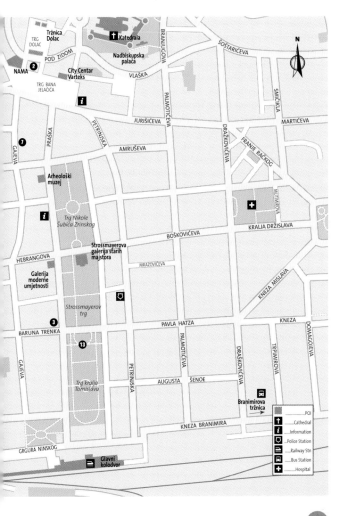

replaced with a monument to socialist women, and the square was renamed Trg Republike (Republic Square). The return of the statue in 1990 marked a symbolic step on the road to Croatian independence. Tram: 1, 6, 11, 12, 13, 14, 17 to Trg bana Jelačića

Trg kralja Tomislava (King Tomislav Square)

Travellers arriving in Zagreb by train are treated to a view of this splendid square as soon as they step out of the station. It is named after Tomislav, who ruled Croatia from AD 910–28 and is considered the first Croatian king. A statue of Tomislav, on horseback and wielding a sword in his right hand, overlooks the start of the square. Beyond here, sweeping lawns, flowerbeds and a fountain lead the eye to the Umjetnički paviljon (Art Pavilion), a cream-coloured building designed for the Millennium Exhibition in Budapest in 1896 and re-erected two years later in Zagreb.

ART ON THE SQUARE

As you wander around Trg maršala Tita, keep your eyes open for three pieces of sculpture. The first is *Well of Life* by Ivan Meštrović (see page 68), in a sunken pit in front of the National Theatre. There is more Meštrović on the north side of the square, with his seated figure, *History of the Croats*, displayed at the entrance to Zagreb University. Finally, outside the Arts & Crafts Museum, is a statue of *St George Killing the Dragon*, by Anton Fernkorn, who also created the equestrian statue of Baron Josip Jelačić in Trg bana Jelačića.

The front of the building now houses a famous restaurant, Paviljon (see page 92), while the rear half still functions as an art gallery. ⊘ Tram: 2, 4, 6, 9, 13 to Glavni kolodvor

Trg maršala Tita (Marshal Tito Square)

Despite all the changes in Croatia, this imposing square continues to be named after the former Yugoslav leader Tito. It is dominated by the yellow Habsburg façade of the Croatian National Theatre, together with the matching Arts & Crafts Museum. The best place to take in the view is from a seat outside Kazališna kavana café. ⊘ Tram: 12, 13, 14, 17 to Trg maršala Tita

Trg Nikole Šubića Zrinskog (Zrinjevac)

Judging by the number of smooching couples to be found on its benches, the square known as Zrinjevac is easily Zagreb's most romantic park. Try to get here on a Saturday morning in summer, when promenade concerts are held in the bandstand at the centre (see page 46). ⊘ Tram: 6, 13 to Zrinjevac

Trg Petra Preradovića (Flower Square)

This busy square is named after the poet Petra Preradović (1818–72), but everyone calls it Cvjetni trg (Flower Square) because of the flower stalls which lend it a splash of colour throughout the year. These days, it acts as the focus for a lively pedestrianised area with terrace bars and cafés that spill into nearby streets such as Bogovićeva. On the north side of the square, the Serbian Orthodox Church of the Transfiguration is the meeting place of Zagreb's Serb community. ⊘ Tram: 1, 6, 11, 12, 13, 14, 17 to Trg bana Jelačića

CULTURE

Arheološki muzej (Archaeological Museum)

This museum has three floors of displays on Croatian history
and archaeology. Don't miss the Vučedol Dove, a beautiful
ceramic vessel in the shape of a bird, which was made at least
4,000 years ago. It was found near Vukovar, a town devastated
in the recent war, and has since become a symbol of peace. The
other must-see is the so-called Zagreb Mummy, brought back
from Egypt by a Croatian noble in 1848. It was wrapped in a shroud
that on closer inspection turned out to be a manuscript written
in Etruscan: to date it remains the longest known example
of Etruscan text and the only known surviving linen book.

⬤ *The bandstand in Zrinjevac*

SNACK AMONG THE STONES
If you visit the Archaeological Museum in summer, pause for a while in the Lapidarium courtyard café, where you can sip coffee in a pleasant garden surrounded by Roman statuary, sarcophagi and stones.

🅐 Trg Nikole Šubića Zrinskog 19 🅣 01 487 3101 🆆 www.amz.hr
🅣 10.00–17.00 Tues, Wed & Fri, 10.00–22.00 Thur, 10.00–13.00 Sat & Sun 🅝 Tram: 6, 13 to Zrinjevac. Admission charge

Etnografski muzej (Ethnographic Museum)
Housed in an art nouveau building with stained glass and sculptures on the façade, this museum features traditional costumes and artefacts from Croatia and abroad. The upper floor is devoted to Croatia, with richly embroidered clothes from various regions of the country, along with jewellery and musical instruments. The ground floor features non-European cultures, with Native American headdresses, African masks, Aboriginal bark paintings and Japanese samurai swords. 🅐 Mažuranićev trg 14 🅣 01 482 6220 🆆 www.mdc.hr/etno 🅛 10.00–18.00 Tues–Thur, 10.00–13.00 Fri–Sun 🅝 Tram: 12, 13, 14, 17 to Trg maršala Tita. Admission charge

Galerija moderne umjetnosti (Modern Gallery)
This pristine art gallery provides a broad overview of Croatian art since the late 19th century, beginning with large canvases by Dalmatian artist Vlaho Bukovac (1855–1922). Other works

include studies by Anton Fernkorn for his public statues of Josip
Jelačić and George and the Dragon in Zagreb, naïve art from
Hlebine and large abstract paintings by Edo Murtić (1921–2005).
🅐 Hebrangova 1 🕿 01 492 2368 🕔 10.00–18.00 Tues–Fri, 10.00–13.00
Sat & Sun 🚋 Tram: 6, 13 to Zrinjevac. Admission charge

Muzej Mimara (Mimara Museum)

This wide-ranging museum owes its existence to one man with
a lifelong passion for collecting. The businessman Ante Topić
Mimara (1898–1987) spent much of his vast fortune acquiring
works of art, which he donated to the nation before his death.

🔺 *Deep in thought: Meštrović's statue of Strossmayer*

His tastes varied from Egyptian glass and Persian carpets to Ming vases, Italian Renaissance sculpture and French Impressionists, so there is something for everyone here. ⓐ Rooseveltov Trg 4 ⓣ 01 482 8100 ⓛ 10.00–17.00 Tues, Wed, Fri & Sat, 10.00–19.00 Thur, 10.00–14.00 Sun ⓝ Tram: 12, 13, 14, 17 to Trg maršala Tita. Admission charge

Muzej za umjetnost i obrt (Arts & Crafts Museum)

With collections of glassware, ceramics, clocks and watches, photography, sacred art, Jewish devotional items and 20th-century design, this museum certainly takes a broad view of the arts. The first floor is devoted to furniture and tapestries from the houses of the Croatian nobility. ⓐ Trg maršala Tita 10 ⓣ 01 488 2111 ⓦ www.muo.hr ⓛ 10.00–19.00 Tues, Wed, Fri & Sat, 10.00–22.00 Thur, 10.00–14.00 Sun ⓝ Tram: 12, 13, 14, 17 to Trg maršala Tita. Admission charge

Strossmayerova galerija starih majstora (Strossmayer Gallery)

This gallery of paintings from the 15th to 19th centuries is based on the collection of Josip Juraj Strossmayer (1815–1905), a bishop, politician, art patron and campaigner for Croat-Serb unity. It includes works by some of the leading European artists, including Bellini, Carpaccio and El Greco. It is housed on the second floor of the Croatian Academy of Sciences and Arts, founded by Strossmayer in 1880. Look in the entrance lobby for the Baška Stone, an 11th-century tablet from the island of Krk containing the earliest known example of the Glagolitic script, a 41-letter alphabet used in Croatia for 1,000 years. A statue by Ivan Meštrović – of Strossmayer in pensive pose – stands outside

the building. ⓐ Trg Nikole Šubića Zrinskog 11 ⓣ 01 489 5117
ⓦ www.mdc.hr/strossmayer ⓛ 10.00–13.00, 17.00–19.00 Tues,
10.00–13.00 Wed–Sun ⓝ Tram: 6, 13 to Zrinjevac. Admission charge

RETAIL THERAPY

Ilica is the Oxford Street of Zagreb, lined with clothes and shoe
shops of varying quality. Some of the best are found close to Trg
bana Jelačića, such as high-street fashion chains **Heruc Galerija**
(ⓐ No. 26) and **Image Haddad** (ⓐ Nos. 6 and 21). Also here is the
historic department store **Nama** (ⓐ No. 4).

Algoritam The bookshop beneath Hotel Dubrovnik has a wide
range of English-language books and magazines. ⓐ Gajeva 1
ⓣ 01 481 8672 ⓛ 08.30–21.00 Mon–Fri, 08.30–15.00 Sat
ⓝ Tram: 1, 6, 11, 12, 13, 14, 17 to Trg bana Jelačića

Aquarius The best place to buy CDs in Zagreb, from the latest pop
releases to Croatian folk, jazz, classical and rock. ⓐ Varšavska 13
ⓣ 01 639 1673 ⓛ 08.00–20.00 Mon–Fri, 08.00–15.00 Sat
ⓝ Tram: 1, 6, 11, 12, 13, 14, 17 to Trg bana Jelačića, or tram: 12, 13,
14, 17 to Frankopanska

Bakina kuća This lovely little gift shop near Zrinjevac Park
sells Croatian wines, spirits, honey, natural cosmetics and
high-class souvenirs. ⓐ Strossmayerov trg 7 ⓣ 01 485 2525
ⓛ 09.00–19.30 ⓝ Tram: 2, 4, 6, 9, 13 to Glavni kolodvor,
or tram: 6, 13 to Zrinjevacc

Britanski trg During the week, a farmers' market is held on this square, but on Sunday mornings it becomes a lively antiques fair, with traders selling everything from jewellery and pottery to old coins and household junk. ⓐ Britanski trg ⓒ 08.00–14.00 Sun ⓝ Tram: 1, 6, 11 to Britanski trg

Croata This is the place to come for a silk tie, scarf or cravat (see page 24). The shop is situated inside the Oktogon precinct, a charming Viennese-style shopping arcade built in 1899 with a stained-glass dome at the centre. ⓐ Ilica 5 ⓣ 01 481 2726 ⓦ www.croata.hr ⓒ 08.00–20.00 Mon–Fri, 08.00–15.00 Sat ⓝ Tram: 1, 6, 11, 12, 13, 14, 17 to Trg bana Jelačića

Dancing Bear This small, independent record shop sells music by Croatian artists. ⓐ Gundulićeva 7 ⓣ 01 483 0850 ⓒ 09.00–20.00 Mon–Fri, 09.00–15.00 Sat ⓝ Tram: 12, 13, 14, 17 to Frankopanska

Etno-butik Mara Handmade cotton clothing, bags and belts embroidered with traditional Croatian designs are on sale at this small boutique. ⓐ Ilica 49 ⓣ 01 480 6511 ⓒ 09.00–20.00 Mon–Fri, 09.00–14.30 Sat ⓝ Tram: 2, 6, 11 to Frankopanska

Franja This upmarket coffee shop and delicatessen sells a wide range of Croatian goodies, including wines, spirits, liqueurs and olive oils. ⓐ Ilica 24 ⓣ 01 483 0189 ⓒ 07.00–21.00 Mon–Fri, 07.00–20.00 Sat, 09.00–15.00 Sun ⓝ Tram: 1, 6, 11, 12, 13, 14, 17 to Trg bana Jelačića

Nama Housed in a 19th-century building on a corner of the main square, Narodni Magazin (People's Store) was the leading department store in Yugoslavia. These days, it is looking a little careworn. ⓐ Ilica 4 ☎ 01 480 3111 ⏱ 08.00–20.30 Mon–Fri, 08.00–15.00 Sat Ⓝ Tram: 1, 6, 11, 12, 13, 14, 17 to Trg bana Jelačića

Natura Croatica Everything here is made in Croatia using natural ingredients, from wild bear salami to lavender honey, pepper biscuits, quince brandy and sheep's cheese in olive oil. ⓐ Preradovićeva 8 ☎ 01 485 5076 ⏱ 09.00–21.00 Mon–Fri, 10.00–16.00 Sat Ⓝ Tram: 1, 6, 11, 12, 13, 14, 17 to Trg bana Jelačića, or tram: 6, 13 to Zrinjevac

Profil Megastore The nearest thing in Zagreb to a US-style bookstore, with three floors of books, music, films, computer games and an internet café. ⓐ Bogovićeva 7 ☎ 01 487 7300 ⏱ 09.00–22.00 Mon–Sat Ⓝ Tram: 1, 6, 11, 12, 13, 14, 17 to Trg bana Jelačića

Udruga hrvatski suvenir Next door to Etno-butik Mara (see page 87), this small shop sells original souvenirs from Croatian artists. ⓐ Ilica 50 ☎ 01 480 6512 ⏱ 14.00–19.00 Tues & Thur, 10.00–15.00 Mon, Wed & Fri Ⓝ Tram: 2, 6, 11 to Frankopanska

Valentino moda Pick up a Croatian football shirt or a Dinamo Zagreb cap for the football fan in your life at this sports shop beside the tourist office. ⓐ Jurišićeva 1 ☎ 01 481 3401 ⏱ 10.00–20.00 Mon–Fri, 09.00–14.00 Sat Ⓝ Tram: 1, 6, 11, 12, 13, 14, 17 to Trg bana Jelačića

Varteks City Centar This department store on the main square has five floors of perfumes, cosmetics, men's and women's fashions and CDs. ⓐ Trg bana Jelačića 8 ⓘ 01 489 3105 ⓛ 09.00–20.30 Mon–Fri, 09.00–17.00 Sat ⓝ Tram: 1, 6, 11, 12, 13, 14, 17 to Trg bana Jelačića

TAKING A BREAK

Ham-Ham £ ❶ Fast food with a difference – choose from homemade vegetarian soups, sandwiches, burgers, croquettes and freshly prepared salads, then take them outside to a courtyard with funky furniture and cool music. ⓐ Varšavska 8 ⓘ 01 483 0483 ⓛ 09.00–23.00 Mon–Thur, 09.00–01.00 Fri & Sat ⓝ Tram: 1, 6, 11, 12, 13, 14, 17 to Trg bana Jelačića

Mala kavana £ ❷ You can take your pick of the cafés on the main square, but this is always a good choice, with sandwiches, ice cream and a tempting selection of pastries as well as excellent coffee and hot chocolate. ⓐ Trg bana Jelačića 5 ⓘ 01 481 6833 ⓛ 08.00–23.00 ⓝ Tram: 1, 6, 11, 12, 13, 14, 17 to Trg bana Jelačića

Palace £ ❸ With chandeliers, polished wood and a tinkling piano in the evenings, the ground-floor café of the Palace Hotel is a throwback to 19th-century Vienna and is the place to take anyone you want to impress. Try the house speciality *štrukli* (cottage cheese pastry). ⓐ Strossmayerov trg 10 ⓘ 01 489 9600 ⓛ 08.00–23.00 ⓝ Tram: 2, 4, 6, 9, 13 to Glavni kolodvor

Tip-Top £ ❹ This traditional Dalmatian tavern serves some of the best-value food in Zagreb, with daily lunchtime specials of lamb with peas, salt cod, fish casserole and octopus goulash served on different days of the week. ⓐ Gundulićeva 18 ⓣ 01 483 0349 ⓛ 07.00–22.00 Mon–Sat ⓝ Tram: 1, 6, 11, 12, 13, 14, 17 to Trg bana Jelačića

Vallis Aurea £ ❺ This pub by the lower funicular station is a good place for a filling lunch, with tables on the terrace or in a folksy interior with dark wood and check tablecloths. It serves the spicy home cooking of Slavonia, with daily specials ranging from boiled beef with horseradish to wine goulash. ⓐ Tomićeva 4 ⓣ 01 483 1305 ⓛ 09.00–23.00 Mon–Sat ⓝ Tram: 1, 6, 11, 12, 13, 14, 17 to Trg bana Jelačića

Vincek £ ❻ A temple to all things sweet, from gorgeous gateaux to irresistible ice-cream sundaes. There are more ice-cream parlours on nearby Bogovićeva. ⓐ Ilica 18 ⓣ 01 483 3612 ⓛ 08.30–23.00 ⓝ Tram: 1, 6, 11, 12, 13, 14, 17 to Trg bana Jelačića

Boban ££ ❼ Owned by former Croatian football star Zvonimir Boban, this busy cellar restaurant near the main square serves a largely Italian menu of pasta and salads. The tagliatelle with Istrian truffles is a treat. ⓐ Gajeva 9 ⓣ 01 481 1549 ⓛ 10.00–00.00 ⓝ Tram: 1, 6, 11, 12, 13, 14, 17 to Trg bana Jelačića

Hrvatski kulturni klub ££ ❽ With comfy leather armchairs in the basement of the Arts & Crafts Museum, the 'Croatian Culture Club' feels more like an old-fashioned gentlemen's club than a restaurant. You can sit out of doors in a pretty courtyard in summer. ⓐ Trg maršala Tita 10 ⓣ 01 482 8084 ⓛ 10.00–00.00 Mon–Sat ⓝ Tram: 12, 13, 14, 17 to Trg maršala Tita

K Pivovari ££ ❾ This large beer hall is set in the grounds of the Ožujsko brewery, with tables out in the garden in summer. Choose from classic pub fare such as sausages, steaks and grilled meat, washed down with local beer. ⓐ Ilica 222 ⓣ 01 375 1808 ⓛ 10.00–00.00 Mon–Sat, 10.00–17.00 Sun ⓝ Tram: 2, 6, 11 to Mandaličina

AFTER DARK

RESTAURANTS
Mašklin i Lata ££ ❿ Hidden away behind the unpromising façade of the Old Pharmacy pub, this smart cellar restaurant is the best place to try Dalmatian specialities such as Pag sheep's cheese, black squid ink risotto, *pašticada* (veal stew with gnocchi) and grilled fish with *blitva* (Swiss chard). ⓐ Hebrangova 11A ⓣ 01 481 8273 ⓛ 09.00–23.00 Mon–Sat ⓝ Tram: 6, 13 to Zrinjevac

Vinodol ££ ⓫ Classic Croatian meat dishes, including spit-roast lamb and veal cooked under a metal lid, are served in a cavernous brick-vaulted dining room or in a candlelit garden on summer evenings. ⓐ Teslina 10 ⓣ 01 481 1427 ⓛ 10.00–00.00 ⓝ Tram: 6, 13 to Zrinjevac, or tram: 1, 6, 11, 12, 13, 14, 17 to Trg bana Jelačića

Gallo £££ ⓬ Walk through the door of a mustard-yellow apartment block in Zagreb's business district and you come to this attractive courtyard restaurant, which serves several varieties of homemade pasta plus fresh fish and seafood specialities including octopus carpaccio and shellfish risotto. ⓐ Hebrangova 34 ⓣ 01 481 4014 ⓦ www.gallo.hr ⓛ 12.00–00.00 ⓝ Tram: 6, 13 to Zrinjevac

Paviljon £££ ⓭ Dress up for dinner at this celebrated restaurant, in the refined setting of the 19th-century Art Pavilion. The service is faultless, the food is a blend of Croatian and Mediterranean, and you can enjoy modern art on the walls as you dine. It's well worth trying the signature dish of crispy roast duck on a bed of red cabbage and figs. In summer, you can eat outside on the terrace. ⓐ Trg kralja Tomislava 22 ⓣ 01 481 3066 ⓦ www.restaurant-paviljon.com ⓛ 12.00–00.00 Mon–Sat ⓝ Tram: 2, 4, 6, 9, 13 to Trg bana Jelačića

BARS & CLUBS

BP Club Some of Croatia's finest jazz musicians appear at the BP Club, whose owner, legendary vibraphone player Boško Petrović, is still performing regularly in his 70s. There is live jazz and blues most nights. ⓐ Teslina 7 ⓣ 01 481 4444 ⓦ www.bpclub.hr ⓛ 10.00–02.00 Mon–Sat, 17.00–02.00 Sun ⓝ Tram: 6, 13 to Zrinjevac

Jazz Club This cellar bar opened in 2006 as a platform for young musicians from the nearby Music Academy. The music ranges from funky modern jazz to late-night sultry jazz standards. Unlike in other clubs, there is no cover charge. ⓐ Gundulićeva 11 ⓛ 07.00–00.00 ⓝ Tram: 12, 13, 14, 17 to Frankopanska

Sax Run by the Croatian Musicians' Union, this garage-like club has live music almost every night. You can catch jazz on Wednesdays, soul on Thursdays, plus local and visiting pop acts. ⓐ Palmotićeva 22 ⓘ 01 487 2836 ⓦ www.sax-zg.hr ⓛ 09.00–04.00 ⓝ Tram: 4, 8, 11, 12, 14 to Draškovićeva

Škola Climb the stairs above a bookshop to this ultra-trendy penthouse bar, set in an old school where 'everything is white except the plants'. With cool cocktails, Japanese-inspired fusion food, a roof terrace and chairs which resemble futuristic space capsules, Škola started the design bar trend when it opened in 2002 and it continues to set the standard for others to follow. ⓐ Bogovićeva 7 ⓘ 01 482 8196 ⓦ www.skolaloungebar.com ⓛ 10.00–01.00 Mon–Sat, 11.00–00.00 Sun ⓝ Tram: 1, 6, 11, 12, 13, 14, 17 to Trg bana Jelačića

CLASSICAL MUSIC
Hrvatski glazbeni zavod (Croatian Music Institute) This 19th-century concert hall hosts regular recitals of chamber and classical music. ⓐ Gundulićeva 6 ⓘ 01 483 0822 ⓛ Box office: 11.00–13.00 Mon–Fri and one hour before performance ⓝ Tram: 1, 6, 11, 12, 13, 14, 17 to Trg bana Jelačića

THEATRE
Hrvatsko narodno kazalište (Croatian National Theatre) Zagreb's principal venue for drama, ballet and opera – get to a show here if you can. ⓐ Trg maršala Tita 15 ⓘ 01 482 8532 ⓦ www.hnk.hr ⓛ Box office: 10.00–14.00 Mon–Fri and 90 minutes before performance ⓝ Tram: 12, 13, 14, 17 to Trg maršala Tita

Outside the centre

Although Gornji grad and Donji grad have enough to keep
you busy for days, it would be a pity to leave Zagreb without
discovering what lies beyond the city centre. The biggest draws
are Maksimir Park and Mount Medvednica, but lesser-known
sights include Zagreb's biggest flea market at Hrelić and the
peaceful cemetery at Mirogoj. All of these sights can easily
be reached by bus or tram from the centre.

SIGHTS & ATTRACTIONS

Bundek

This artificial lake was created in 1960 when gravel was dug for
the construction of Most slobode (Freedom Bridge) across the
River Sava. In fact, it resembles a pair of lakes, linked by a narrow
channel and crossed by a wooden footbridge. During the 1960s,
when seaside holidays were still a luxury, Bundek became a
popular bathing spot known as *Zagrebačko more* (Zagreb Sea)
but it gradually fell into disuse. The entire area was re-landscaped
in 2006 with pebble beaches, gardens, a lakeside café and a
children's playground and it is once again crowded with local

WHAT'S IN A NAME?

The origins of the name Bundek are rather macabre –
it was the surname of a young boy who drowned in the
lake soon after it first opened.

families on summer afternoons. You can swim in the large lake, fish in the smaller one or follow the footpath that runs around the shore. Take the bus from behind the railway station and get off at the first stop after crossing the River Sava. Bus: 219, 220, 221, 268 to Hipodrom

Jarun

On hot summer days, cool off by visiting Jarun, a large lake beside the River Sava. Created for the 1987 World University Games in Zagreb, it is now a popular venue for outdoor sports and relaxation. There are facilities for rowing, canoeing, windsurfing, tennis, beach volleyball and mini-golf, and the entire lake is surrounded by a 6-km (4-mile) cycle path used by walkers, joggers and skaters.

● *Relax with the locals at Jarun*

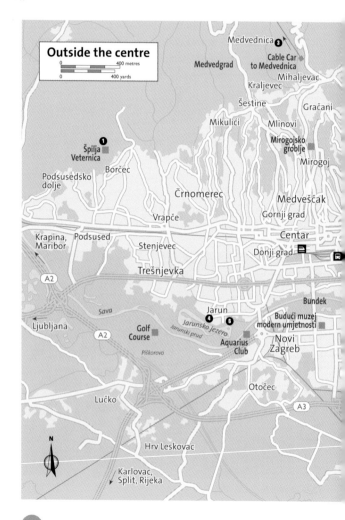

Outside the centre

0 — 400 metres
0 — 400 yards

Medvednica ❸

Medvedgrad

Cable Car
to Medvednica

Mihaljevac

Kraljevec

Šestine

Gračani

Mikulići

Mlinovi

Špilja ❶
Veternica

Mirogojsko
groblje

Borčec

Mirogoj

Podsusedsko
dolje

Črnomerec

Medveščak

Vrapče

Gornji grad

Krapina,
Maribor

Podsused

Centar

Stenjevec

Donji grad

Trešnjevka

A2

Bundek

Sava

Jarun

Buduči muzej
modern umjetnosti

Ljubljana

A2

Golf
Course

Jarunsko jezero
Jarunski prud

❹ ❺

Novi
Zagreb

Piškorovo

Aquarius
Club

Lučko

Otočec

A3

N

Hrv Leskovac

Karlovac,
Split, Rijeka

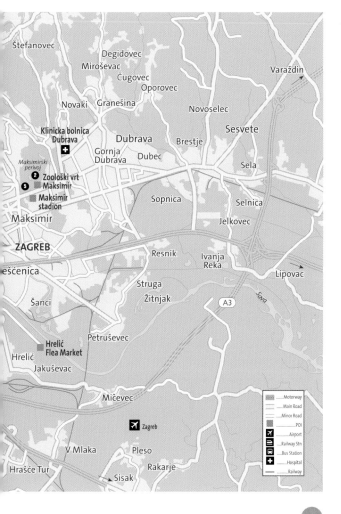

There are several beaches, with lifeguards and showers, and a small nudist beach on the southern shore. To escape the crowds, head for one of the islands on the lake, peaceful nature reserves attracting fishermen and birds. Malo jezero (Small Lake), at the eastern end, is a lovely spot, with cafés and bars scattered around a wide arc of pebble beach. The Avenue of Croatian Sporting Greats, on the north shore, has panels depicting sporting heroes such as tennis player Goran Ivanišević and the stars of the 1998 World Cup football team. ⓣ Tram: 5, 17 to Jarun

Maksimirski perivoj (Maksimir Park)

Maksimir Park is Zagreb's weekend playground, a place to relax, walk, picnic, feed the swans, fall asleep on the grass or take your children to the zoo. Laid out in 1794 with footpaths, bridges and lakes, it is one of the oldest public parks in Europe. It is filled with charming 19th-century follies such as the Echo Pavilion and Swiss House, as well as the Vidikovac, a romantic three-storey belvedere perched on a hill at the end of the main avenue. Kids will enjoy the nearby zoo, Zoološki vrt Maksimir (see page 134). Across the

MUSIC THERAPY

When one of the elephants at Maksimir Zoo died in 2006, the surviving elephant, Suma, was stricken with grief – until the zookeepers organised a concert of classical music outside her cage. The music had such a calming effect that speakers have now been installed and you can see Suma relaxing while listening to Mozart each morning and afternoon.

road, Maksimir stadion is the home of Dinamo Zagreb and the Croatian national football team. www.park-maksimir.hr
 Tram: 4, 7, 11, 12 to Bukovačka

Medvednica

When the heat of the city gets too much, escape to the cool of Medvednica (Bear Mountain), whose shady pine woods provide welcome relief in summer. Getting there is an adventure in itself. Take the bus from tram terminus at Mihaljevac and enjoy the winding ride to the *žičara* (cable car) station for the spectacular 20-minute ascent to the summit (on the hour from 08.00–20.00).

You arrive at the Tomislavov dom hotel beneath the summit of Sljeme, around 1,000 m (3,280 ft) above sea level, with views over the rural Zagorje region to the north. From here, there is a wide choice of hiking paths, but the easiest descent is to take trail 26 from the car park of the Tomislavov Dom hotel and follow it for around 30 minutes to the Grafičar mountain hut. Nearby is **Rudnik Zrinski** (Zrinski Mine 10.00–16.00 Sat & Sun; closed Sat in July & Aug), a reconstructed silver mine where you can walk through the underground corridors and learn about the history of mining on Medvednica. The path continues with a right fork leading to Medvedgrad, a restored 13th-century fortress with views over Zagreb. Eventually you arrive in the village of Šestine, where you can catch a bus back to Zagreb. During the winter, there is skiing on the slopes of Sljeme and you can hire skis and equipment near the summit. 01 458 6317
 www.pp-medvednica.hr Tram 15 to Mihaljevac followed by bus to Tomislavov dom

Mirogojsko groblje (Mirogoj Cemetery)

Not many cemeteries are also tourist attractions, but Mirogoj would be worth a visit even without the interest caused by the recent war. As you stroll along its avenues, it is fascinating to look at the tombstones, with their Catholic, Orthodox, Jewish, Muslim and Communist symbols revealing the diversity of the people who have lived and died in Zagreb. Many of Croatia's

🔺 *The Renaissance arcades at Mirogoj*

noble families have their tombs in the elegant Renaissance arcades to either side of the main entrance, designed by the architect of the cathedral, Hermann Bollé, whose bust stands outside. With finely carved memorials by artists including Ivan Meštrović, Mirogoj is an open-air museum of funerary sculpture. The black granite tomb of Croatia's first president, Franjo Tuđman (1922–99), is always covered in flowers and candles. Outside the main gate is a memorial park to the victims of the 1991–5 Homeland War, with a sculpture inscribed with the names of 13,500 dead. The monument incorporates the Zid boli (Wall of Pain), a structure composed of bricks, each of which represents a missing person and which were originally placed by the victims' families on a street corner in Zagreb. Ⓝ Bus: 106 from Kaptol

Špilja Veternica (Veternica Cave)

Follow the signs uphill from the end of the bus line at Gornji Stenjevec, where a steep path through the forest leads to this underground cave, part of the Medvednica Nature Park. Almost 7 km (4½ miles) has been explored by speleologists, but only a small section is open to visitors and it can only be seen on guided tours. Take warm clothing even in summer, as the air is a constant 8°C (46°F) inside, and wear good shoes as it can get slippery. Skeletons of bears, rhino, leopards and hyena have been found in the cave, and bats still hibernate here in winter. A short climb leads to the Glavica mountain hut (see page 102). ☎ 01 458 6317 Ⓦ www.pp-medvednica.hr ⏱ 10.00–16.00 Sat & Sun, May–Oct (last entry 15.10); closed Sat in July & Aug Ⓝ Bus: 124 from Črnomerec to Gornji Stenjevec

RETAIL THERAPY

For a taste of the old Yugoslavia, take a bus or shared taxi from behind the railway station, or walk along the raised embankment of the River Sava, to the Sunday morning flea market at Hrelić in Novi Zagreb. You arrive at what looks like a giant car park but is in fact a second-hand car market. Head further into the mêlée and you will find stalls selling goods from cheap jeans and trainers to books and CDs. Cafés sell hearty Balkan food such as spit-roast pork and huge vats of bean stew. Ⓝ Bus: 295 to Sajam Jakuševec

TAKING A BREAK

Planinarski dom "Glavica" £ ❶ Keep walking for ten minutes beyond Veternica Cave to reach this busy mountain refuge, one of several within the Medvednica Nature Park. Choose from rustic mountain fare such as sausages and *grah* (bean soup), then eat it outside on the terrace with views over Zagreb. ⓐ Medvednica ❶ 01 481 8551 Ⓦ www.pp-medvednica.hr Ⓛ 09.00–22.00 Tues–Sun

Vidikovac £ ❷ The belvedere at the centre of Maksimir Park is now a delightful café, whose terrace provides the perfect vantage point overlooking the park. ⓐ Maksimirski perivoj bb ❶ 01 230 8204 Ⓛ 08.00–21.00 Ⓝ Tram: 4, 7, 11, 12 to Bukovačka

Zlatni medvjed £ ❸ This cosy alpine lodge at the summit of Sljeme has log fires in winter and an open-air terrace in summer. It serves hearty mountain dishes such as sausages, venison goulash and meat cooked on an outdoor grill.

ⓐ Medvednica ⓣ 091 504 9466 ⓛ 09.00–22.00 Tues–Sun
ⓝ Tram: 15 to Mihaljevac followed by bus

Jarunski dvori ££ ❹ This pub on the north shore of Lake Jarun serves a menu of grilled meat and other Croatian classics.
ⓐ Aleja Matije Ljubeka bb ⓣ 01 383 1672 ⓛ 09.00–00.00 Mon–Sat, 09.00–22.00 Sun ⓝ Tram: 5, 17 to Jarun

Maksimir ££ ❺ The restaurant at the entrance to Maksimir Park serves standard Croatian cuisine. ⓐ Maksimirski perivoj bb ⓣ 01 231 0210 ⓛ 08.00–22.00 Mar–Oct, 09.00–18.00 Nov–Feb ⓝ Tram: 4, 7, 11, 12 to Bukovačka

AFTER DARK

RESTAURANTS
Lido £££ ❻ Dine on fresh fish and seafood at this chic waterfront restaurant with great views over Lake Jarun. It is situated at the heart of Jarun's busy nightlife scene, so you don't have to go far for after-dinner dancing and drinks. ⓐ Malo jezero, Jarun bb ⓣ 01 383 2837 ⓛ 10.00–00.00 ⓝ Tram: 5, 17 to Horvati

BARS & CLUBS
Aquarius Zagreb's biggest club began as a wooden shack on the shores of Lake Jarun, but now spreads over two dance floors with room for over 1,000 people. At night it pulsates to the sounds of hip-hop and electronic grooves, plus performances from big-name live acts. ⓐ Aleja Matije Ljubeka bb ⓣ 01 364 0231 ⓦ www.aquarius.hr ⓛ 22.00–06.00 ⓝ Tram: 5, 17 to Horvati

Dublin Pub This large Irish pub close to Maksimir Park has Croatian and Irish beers and a simple menu of pub food. There is live jazz on Thursday nights, plus DJs and karaoke at weekends. ⓐ Maksimirska 75 ⓣ 01 236 0493 ⓛ 08.00–01.00 Sun–Thur, 08.00–02.00 Fri & Sat ⓝ Tram: 4, 7, 11, 12 to Jordanovac

Gallery With sofas for chilling out on the terrace and cool sounds from top international DJs, Gallery is attracting the smart set. Dress up if you want to get in here at weekends. ⓐ Aleja Mira ⓣ 091 113 3221 ⓛ 10.00–01.00 Sun–Thur, 10.00–04.00 Fri & Sat ⓝ Tram: 5, 17 to Horvati

Movie Pub This themed pub near the River Sava has photos of film stars and Hollywood memorabilia on the walls. There is live music most nights and the karaoke parties on Wednesday and Thursday attract a lively student crowd. ⓐ Savska Cesta 141 ⓣ 01 605 5045 ⓛ 07.00–02.00 Mon–Wed, 07.00–04.00 Thur–Sat, 18.00–02.00 Sun ⓝ Tram: 4, 5, 14, 17 to Prisavlje

CLASSICAL MUSIC

Koncertna Dvorana Vatroslav Lisinski (Vatroslav Lisinski Concert Hall) Zagreb's prestige venue for classical music is home to the Zagreb Philharmonic Orchestra and also hosts jazz and world music concerts. ⓐ Trg Stjepana Radića 4 ⓣ 01 612 1167 ⓦ www.lisinski.hr ⓛ Box office open 09.00–20.00 Mon–Fri, 09.00–14.00 Sat and one hour before performance ⓝ Tram: 3, 5, 13 to Lisinski

▶ *The baroque beauty of Varaždin*

Samobor

With pastel-coloured 19th-century houses around a pretty main square, a stream running through the centre and the whole scene overlooked by a handsome onion-domed church, Samobor is the perfect picture-postcard provincial town. No wonder, then, that at weekends it is packed out by day-trippers from Zagreb, who seem to spend most of their time in cafés enjoying the local speciality, *samoborska kremšnita* – a delicious custard tart between layers of flaky pastry. Garlic sausages and mustard are also big on the menu, making Samobor something of a gastronomic pilgrimage. Just 20 km (12 miles) from Zagreb, you can visit Samobor for lunch and be back in time for tea.

GETTING THERE

Buses for Samobor leave roughly every 30 minutes from a stop at the back of the central bus station in Zagreb. The journey takes 45 minutes and you can buy your ticket on the bus. There are also less frequent but slightly faster buses to Samobor from the tram terminals at Črnomerec and Ljubljanica.

TOURIST INFORMATION
The tourist office on the main square has maps, postcards and English-speaking staff. ❷ Trg kralja Tomislava 5 ❶ 01 336 0044 ❸ 09.00–17.00 Mon–Fri

SIGHTS & ATTRACTIONS

Stari grad (Old town)

Samobor is surrounded by wooded hills and you can work up an appetite by taking a walk. From behind the church, Ulica svete Ane climbs past the town cemetery to Anindol, where forest paths lead to the pilgrim chapels of svete Ana (St Anne) and sveti Juraj (St George). Eventually you arrive at Stari grad and the romantically overgrown ruins of a 13th-century castle, all that remains of the free market town of Samobor established by royal charter in 1242.

Trg kralja Tomislava (King Tomislav Square)

Everything in Samobor revolves around the main square, surrounded by baroque townhouses and cafés with a public

● *The parish church and market square*

Zagreb region

0   50 km
0   25 miles

fountain at the centre. The architectural harmony of the square is broken only by the art nouveau pharmacy on the south side, with striking winged angels on its façade. Near here is the parish church, in bold mustard yellow with a tall, onion-domed spire. Behind the church is a peaceful memorial garden to the victims of the Homeland War. The pretty little Gradna brook runs beneath the church, criss-crossed by wooden bridges in an area known as Mala Venecija (Little Venice).

⬤ *Ferdo Livadić, whose home now contains the Town Museum*

CULTURE

Gradski muzej (Town Museum)

This small museum occupies the former townhouse of Ferdo
Livadić, a 19th-century composer and key figure in the Croatian
National Revival. Among the aristocratic portraits and furniture,
look out for a penny-farthing bicycle, ridden by its owner to Trieste
in 1887. A room on the ground floor contains a scale model of
Samobor in 1764, before the town was destroyed by fire; the
only buildings that remain today are the museum and parish
church. There are good riverside walks in the park behind the
museum. ⓐ Livadićeva 7 ⓣ 01 336 1014 ⓒ 09.00–15.00 Tues–Fri,
09.00–13.00 Sat & Sun. Admission charge

Muzej Marton

This privately owned museum has extensive collections of
Biedermeier furniture, porcelain, paintings and clocks in a
19th-century manor house above the church. ⓐ Jurjevska 7
ⓣ 01 332 6426 ⓦ www.muzej-marton.hr ⓒ 10.00–13.00 Sat
& Sun, summer only; at other times by arrangement.
Admission charge

RETAIL THERAPY

You cannot visit Samobor without taking home a jar of the local
mustard or a bottle of *bermet*. For more down-to-earth treats,
the farmers' market near the bus station has stalls selling fruit,
vegetables, flowers, eggs, cheese, yogurt and milk.

Aromatica Herbal cosmetics, soaps and essential oils from Adriatic plants. ⓐ Perkovčeva 14 ⓣ 01 332 4123 ⓛ 11.00–20.00 Mon, 09.00–20.00 Tue–Sat, 11.00–19.00 Sun

Filipec Ring the bell to be admitted into this atmospheric wine cellar for a tasting of *bermet*, a vermouth-type aperitif. The same

⏶ *Enjoy a feast at Filipec*

family makes sweet, spicy grape mustard. Both recipes were introduced by Napoleon's troops during an occupation in 1809 and have been handed down ever since. The cellar is found in an alley off the main square, beside Hotel Livadić. ⓐ Stražnička 1A ❶ 01 336 4835 ⓛ 09.00–18.00 Mon–Sat

Srčeko Artist Silva Krajačić sells her handmade souvenirs, including typical heart designs on glass, from a small wooden kiosk beside the Gradna brook. ⓐ Trg kralja Tomislava ❶ 01 336 3585 ⓛ 09.00–13.00, 17.00–19.00 Mon–Fri, 09.00–13.00 Sat

TAKING A BREAK

Cafés around the square serve gateaux, cakes and pastries, plus fruit salad and ice cream in summer, so it is really just a question of taking your pick.

Kavana Livadić £ Take a trip back to 19th-century Vienna in this elegant coffee house, whose marble tables, hatstands and mirrors give it the feel of an Austrian salon. Opened in 1800, it is still the social centre of Samobor. In summer, you can sit outside in a pretty courtyard garden. ⓐ Trg kralja Tomislava 1 ❶ 01 336 5850 ⓛ 08.00–23.00

Lovački rog-Deni £ For a cheap and filling lunch, you can't beat the 'Hunter's Horn', which sells hearty meat and game dishes at rock-bottom prices. Specialities include *česnjovke* (garlic sausages) with fried potatoes. ⓐ Klešićeva 7 ⓛ 06.00–23.00

U prolazu £ Locals say that this café serves the best *kremšnita* in town – and it is hard to disagree. Other choices include scrummy gateaux and chestnut purée with whipped cream. ⓐ Trg kralja Tomislava 5 ⓣ 01 336 6420 ⓛ 07.00–23.00

Samoborska pivnica ££ This cavernous beer hall behind Hotel Livadić has a rustic atmosphere, with low whitewashed arches and waiters in folk costume. Avoid it if you are vegetarian, as the emphasis is firmly on meat, with salami and beef tongue followed by a platter of local sausages to share. ⓐ Šmidhenova 3 ⓣ 01 336 1623 ⓛ 09.00–23.00

AFTER DARK

RESTAURANTS
Pri staroj vuri ££ An 18th-century house near the church has been turned into a delightful restaurant, serving traditional recipes from the Habsburg era as well as simpler choices like soup with *štrukli* (cottage cheese parcels) and sausages with sauerkraut. The walls and shelves are covered with knick-knacks from old clocks to carnival masks. ⓐ Giznik 2 ⓣ 01 336 0548 ⓛ 11.00–23.00 Mon–Sat, 11.00–18.00 Sun

BARS
Café Havana A lively cocktail bar in the centre of town, this has tables on the square and occasional live jazz in the evenings. ⓐ Trg kralja Tomislava 3 ⓣ 01 336 3916 ⓛ 08.00–00.00 Sun–Thur, 08.00–01.00 Fri & Sat

ACCOMMODATION

Hotel Lavica £ Set in an old stable beside the museum and riverside park, this hotel has simply furnished but comfortable rooms. ⓐ Livadićeva 5 ⓣ 01 332 4946 ⓦ www.lavica-hotel.hr

Hotel Livadić £ One of Croatia's most romantic hotels is found in a 19th-century townhouse on the main square. Everything about this hotel oozes antique charm and style, from the big comfy bedrooms with soft beds, rugs and parquet floors to the elegant breakfast room with its satin-red walls and daily feast of pastries and fresh fruit. A stay here costs less than at a 3-star hotel in Zagreb and it would make an excellent base for visiting the city, as long as you don't mind the bus journey into town. ⓐ Trg kralja Tomislava 1 ⓣ 01 336 5850 ⓦ www.hotel-livadic.hr

> ### CARNIVAL IN SAMOBOR
> The first Carnival ball was held in Samobor in 1827, and the town continues to host some of the most colourful festivities in Croatia, with masked dances and parades in the days leading up to Lent. The dates vary each year but Carnival always ends on Shrove Tuesday, with fireworks, bonfires and the ritual burning of the Carnival prince, Fašnik. As they say in Samobor: 'The fools make fools of themselves every day, but the wise only during Carnival.'

Varaždin

Situated around 75 km (47 miles) northeast of Zagreb, Varaždin is an enjoyable county town of baroque palaces, bicycles and cafés in lively, traffic-free streets. Briefly the capital of 18th-century Croatia, it was destroyed by fire and completely rebuilt, giving the centre a harmonious feel. As you wander around the town, keep your eyes peeled for hidden architectural details, from a bare-breasted mermaid above the door of a chocolate shop to a she-bear carved in stone on a church tower. Perhaps as a result of its large student population, Varaždin is a delightfully easy-going town and makes a relaxing day-trip from Zagreb.

GETTING THERE

By rail

There are 14 trains a day from Zagreb to Varaždin. Most are *putnički* (slow trains), which take around 2½ hours to reach Varaždin. Although the train is slower than the bus, this is a lovely journey, travelling around Medvednica and through the rolling countryside of Zagorje. *Brzi* (express) and Intercity trains make the trip in under two hours, but tickets are more expensive and should be reserved in advance. The railway station in Varaždin is around 500 m (¹/₃ mile) from the centre.

By road

Buses for Varaždin leave about once an hour from the central bus station in Zagreb. The journey takes around 1¾ hours. The bus station in Varaždin is a short walk from the centre.

TOURIST INFORMATION
The tourist office is situated near the castle entrance. If you want to explore in depth, buy a copy of the excellent guidebook *Getting To Know Varaždin*. ⓐ Padovca 3 ⓘ 042 210987 ⓘ 08.00–18.00 Mon–Sat, Apr–Oct; 08.00–16.00 Mon–Fri, 10.00–13.00 Sat, Nov–Mar

SIGHTS & ATTRACTIONS

Baroque architecture

The streets around Trg kralja Tomislava are like an open-air museum, with the finest collection of baroque architecture in Croatia. Much of it dates from the late 18th century, when Varaždin was rebuilt after the fire. The gorgeous cream-coloured Patačić Palace on Franjevački Trg was the social centre of Habsburg Varaždin, where grand parties and balls were once held, while the striking pink palace next door is the headquarters of Varaždin county. Near here is the ridiculously pretty Ursuline church, with its pink and white façade and onion-domed spire. Look carefully at another church, St Nicholas, and you will see Varaždin's coat of arms and a sculpture of a she-bear built into the tower.

Grgur Ninski (Gregory of Nin)

The large bronze statue by Ivan Meštrović (see page 68) outside the Franciscan monastery on Franjevački Trg is of Gregory of Nin, a 10th-century bishop from Dalmatia who campaigned for the use of the Croatian language instead of Latin in the Mass. Look

carefully and you will see that the big toe of his left foot glistens more brightly than all the rest – a result of being rubbed by thousands of visitors as a good-luck charm. If you don't mind looking silly, feel free to join in.

Stari grad (Old town & Castle)

To reach the oldest part of Varaždin, cross the drawbridge and pass through a watchtower to arrive at a moated castle, rebuilt in the 16th century as a Renaissance palace. The area around the

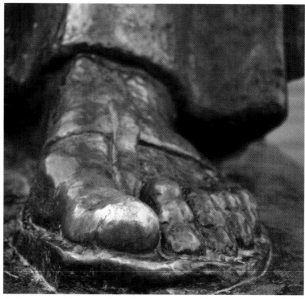

🔺 *Rub Grgur Ninski's toe for good luck*

THE GREAT FIRE
Everyone knows that the Great Fire of London broke out in a bakery, but the fire which destroyed Varaždin in 1776 began when a young farmhand tripped over a pig and dropped his cigar into a haystack, setting off a blaze which rapidly spread through the town. At the time, Varaždin was the Croatian capital, having been chosen by imperial decree nine years earlier. As a result of the fire, the capital moved to Zagreb, and Varaždin's short period in the limelight came to an end.

castle is now a pleasant park and you can walk around the ramparts looking down over the moat. The castle itself has a beautiful galleried courtyard, with displays of old cannons and religious sculpture. The building also contains the **Gradksi muzej** (City Museum ☎ 042 658 754 ⓦ www.gmv.hr), with exhibits on the history of Varaždin and aristocratic furniture from the 16th to 20th centuries. ⓐ Strossmayerovo šetalište ☎ 042 212918 ⓛ 10.00–18.00 Tues–Sun, May–Sept; 10.00–15.00 Tues–Fri, 10.00–13.00 Sat & Sun, Oct–Apr. Admission charge

Trg kralja Tomislava (King Tomislav Square)
This busy square at the centre of town is the heart and soul of Varaždin. It is officially named after the first Croatian king, but everyone calls it Korzo because the terrace bars and cafés are popular meeting places during the evening *korzo* (promenade). At one end is the town hall, with a coat of arms above the

entrance and a distinctive clock tower added in 1791. On the west side of the square, Casa Jaccomini is now the Kraš chocolate shop but it retains some charming 18th-century touches, including the mermaid above the door and the stucco decorations on the ceiling, with the initials of former owner Daniela Jaccomini. Look out too for a figure of an iron man on a corner of a building

● *King Tomislav Square: the heart of Varaždin*

on the south side of the square – this was probably an old blacksmith's shop.

CULTURE

Entomološki muzej (World of Insects)

Housed in the 18th-century Herczer Palace, this small museum contains a fascinating collection of insects, including butterflies, bees, dragonflies and beetles, arranged in subtly lit glass cabinets. ⓐ Franjevački trg 6 ⓣ 042 210474 ⓦ www.mdc.hr ⓛ 10.00–18.00 Tues–Sun, May–Sept; 10.00–15.00 Tues–Fri, 10.00–13.00 Sat & Sun, Oct–Apr. Admission charge

Galerija starih i novih majstora (Gallery of Old & Modern Masters)

This gallery of minor European painting is housed inside the 17th-century Sermage Palace, on a square outside the castle gates. ⓐ Trg Miljenka Stančića 3 ⓣ 042 214172 ⓛ 10.00–18.00 Tues–Sun, May–Sept; 10.00–15.00 Tues–Fri, 10.00–17.00 Sat & Sun, Oct–Apr. Admission charge

THE PURGARI

The Purgari (City Guard) was formed in 1750 and the guards still make an impressive sight in their military uniforms and bearskin hats. On Saturday mornings from May to September, a Changing of the Guard ceremony takes place in front of the town hall at 11.00. The best place to watch it is from a seat outside Kavana Korzo.

RETAIL THERAPY

Traffic is banned from the town centre, so window-shopping is a pleasant experience. Throughout summer and in the build-up to Christmas, artists and craftspeople set up stalls on the streets. The picturesque curving street of Gundulićeva is known as Dućanska (Shopping Street) because it is lined with shops on both sides. At the end of the street is Varteks department store, which has its origins in Varaždin. From Trg kralja Tomislava, Gajeva leads to Trg bana Jelačića, where a busy market is held each morning. You can return to the main square along Uska, a narrow lane of cafés and shops. Centar Mrazović, at the southern end of Trg kralja Tomislava, is a small shopping precinct with art galleries, souvenir shops and the Zalogajćek deli (see page 124).

FESTIVALS

The streets of Varaždin come alive for ten days in August and September during the **Špancirfest** (ⓦ www.spancirfest.com), when free open-air concerts are held in the castle each evening and acrobats, folk dancers and puppet theatre troupes perform in the streets and squares. In recent years, this festival has attracted leading world music artists from countries such as Cuba, Portugal and Scotland. Once the excitement has died down, Varaždin prepares for the **Varaždin Baroque Evenings** (ⓦ www.vbv.hr), when recitals of baroque music in the castle, palaces and churches attract music lovers from Zagreb and beyond.

TAKING A BREAK

Domenico £ This pizzeria is hidden away at the end of a cobbled lane. It offers a simple menu of pizzas, lasagne, spaghetti and salads, served on a terrace overlooking the park in summer.
ⓐ Trg slobode 7 ☎ 042 212017 🕒 08.00–23.00 Mon–Thur, 08.00–00.00 Fri & Sat, 09.00–23.00 Sun

Grenadir £ Tuck into the rustic cuisine of the Zagorje region at this traditional restaurant, which has a few tables out on the street in summer. It's probably best to avoid this place if you're on a diet, as the gut-busting dishes include such delicacies as bread and potato soup and pork steak with bacon and cheese.
ⓐ Kranjčevićeva 12 ☎ 042 211131 🕒 09.00–22.00 Mon–Sat, 12.00–19.00 Sun

🔺 *'Shopping Street': curvy Gundulićeva*

Kavana Korzo £ This Austro-Hungarian coffee house on the main square certainly looks the part, with dark wood, mirrors, chandeliers and comfy red armchairs. The outdoor terrace makes a great spot for people-watching during the evening *korzo*.
ⓐ Trg kralja Tomislava 2 ⓣ 042 320914 ⓛ 08.00–23.00

Mesnica Šanjek £ This butcher is famous for its horsemeat sausages, which you can try in a crusty bread roll filled with mustard. ⓐ Trg slobode 7 ⓣ 042 212731 ⓛ 07.00–20.00 Mon–Fri, 07.00–12.00 Sat

Park £ This old-style restaurant with a large terrace beside the town park serves a standard menu of grilled meat and other Croatian dishes. ⓐ Habdelićeva 6 ⓣ 042 211499 ⓛ 09.00–22.00 Mon–Sat, 10.00–21.00 Sun

Patačić £ Coffee and cakes on the ground floor of the rococo Patačić Palace. ⓐ Franjevački trg 5 ⓣ 042 210938 ⓛ 08.00–23.00

Vindija £ If you fancy a snack, the cafés run by local dairy firm Vindija sell freshly baked baguettes and rolls filled with various cheeses. ⓐ Pavlinska 3; also at Trg slobode 7 ⓣ 042 212687 ⓛ 07.00–20.00 Mon–Sat, 07.30–13.00 Sun

Zalogajček £ This vegetarian café is found in a pretty courtyard off the main square. You can make up your own meal from inexpensive lunchtime specials such as broccoli soup, cheesy potato cakes or spinach burgers with quinoa. Drinks include herbal teas, organic fruit juice, coffee with oat milk, wine and beer. A delicatessen sells Croatian wine, brandy, honey, truffles and olive oil. ⓐ Centar Mrazović, Franjevački trg 1 ❶ 042 200944 🕐 10.00–20.00 Mon–Sat

AFTER DARK

RESTAURANTS
Zlatna guška ££ Recipes from the Austro-Hungarian empire are recreated at this atmospheric cellar restaurant, located in the vaults of a 17th-century palace. Choose from dishes such as nettle soup and the 'daggers of the Counts of Brandenburg': meat and fruit kebabs. ⓐ Habdelićeva 4 ❶ 042 213393 🕐 09.00–23.00

BARS
Aquamarin A trendy student cocktail bar and internet café. ⓐ Gajeva 1 ❶ 042 311868 🕐 07.00–23.00 Mon–Thur, 07.00–02.00 Fri & Sat, 09.00–23.00 Sun

Mea Culpa Billed as Varaždin's first lounge bar, this has sofas, cushions and laid-back music, with a small courtyard garden and a large summer terrace outside the castle gates. ⓐ Padovca 1 ❶ 042 300868 🕐 07.00–00.00 Mon, Tues & Thur, 07.00–01.00 Wed, 07.00–02.00 Fri & Sat, 08.00–00.00 Sun

Sax On the main road near the bus station, Sax has plenty of outdoor seating and occasional live jazz at night. ⓐ Vraza 15 ❶ 042 211509 🕐 07.00–00.00 Mon–Thur, 07.00–01.00 Fri & Sat, 08.00–14.00, 18.00–00.00 Sun

OUT OF TOWN

THEATRE

Hrvatsko narodno kazalište (Croatian National Theatre) This
splendid 19th-century opera house hosts classical music and
drama from September to June. ⓐ Cesarca 1 ⓣ 042 214688
ⓦ www.hnkvz.hr ⓛ Box office opens 10.00–12.00, 18.00–19.30
Mon–Sat and two hours before performance

ACCOMMODATION

For such an attractive town, Varaždin does not have the hotels it
deserves and you are better off visiting as a day-trip from Zagreb.
If you do want to stay overnight, there are three options, all in
the vicinity of the bus station.

Garestin £ Just 25 beds in an old family house converted into
a small hotel. The same owners run the Grenadir and Park
restaurants in town. ⓐ Zagrebačka 34 ⓣ 042 214314
ⓦ www.gastrocom.hr

Hotel Turist £ This old-style Communist hotel has six floors
of comfortable rooms but is somewhat lacking in character.
ⓐ Aleja kralja Zvonimira 1 ⓣ 042 395395 ⓦ www.hotel-turist.hr

Maltar £ This small, friendly, family-run hotel serves an excellent
breakfast. ⓐ Prešernova 1 ⓣ 042 311100 ⓦ www.maltar.hr

ⓘ *Pride of a nation: the Croatian flag*

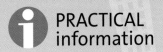

Directory

GETTING THERE

By air

Direct flights from the UK to Zagreb are operated by Croatia Airlines from London Heathrow and Wizzair from Luton. Alternatively, you can fly to another city in Croatia and travel to Zagreb by train or bus. British Airways flies from Gatwick to Dubrovnik and Split, easyJet flies from Bristol and Luton to Rijeka, and Ryanair flies from Stansted to Pula. Budget airlines such as Wizzair, easyJet and Ryanair are established Croatia-bound carriers. If you are prepared to do a little research, you can also seek out cheap flights to cities in neighbouring countries such as Ljubljana and Maribor (Slovenia), or Trieste (Italy), and travel on to Zagreb by bus. The flight time direct from London to Zagreb is around two hours.

British Airways ✆ 0870 850 9850 ⓦ www.britishairways.com
Croatia Airlines ✆ 020 8563 0022 ⓦ www.croatiaairlines.com
easyJet ✆ 0870 600 0000 ⓦ www.easyjet.com
Ryanair ✆ 0871 246 0000 ⓦ www.ryanair.com
Wizzair ✆ 00 48 22 351 9499 ⓦ www.wizzair.com

Many people are aware that air travel emits CO_2, which contributes to climate change. You may be interested in lessening the environmental impact of your flight through the charity **Climate Care** (ⓦ www.climatecare.org), which offsets your CO_2 emissions by funding environmental projects around the world.

By rail

As a major stop on the old Orient Express, Zagreb has good
rail links with Central Europe, with daily trains from Budapest,
Munich, Venice and Vienna. To get there by rail from the UK, you
will need to change trains at least twice. The easiest way to plan
your journey is to consult the monthly *Thomas Cook European
Rail Timetable* (ⓦ www.thomascookpublishing.com). InterRail
passes are valid for journeys to and within Croatia.
Rail Europe ⓣ 0870 837 1371 ⓦ www.raileurope.co.uk

By road

Eurolines operates a weekly service between London Victoria
and Zagreb. The journey time is around 30 hours.
Eurolines ⓣ 0870 514 3219 ⓦ www.eurolines.co.uk

Zagreb is connected to Italy, Hungary and Slovenia by
fast, modern toll motorways. Border crossings are generally
straightforward. In addition to your passport, you may have to
show your driving licence, vehicle registration and insurance
certificate, plus rental documents in the case of a hire car. It is
vital to arrange full insurance before you leave home and to
check that it is valid in Croatia. All vehicles entering Croatia
are required to carry a first-aid kit, emergency warning triangle,
reflective jacket and replacement bulbs. Drive on the right.

Headlights must be switched on at all times. Seatbelts
are compulsory and children under 12 must sit in the rear seat.
It is illegal to use a mobile phone while driving. There is a low
tolerance of drink driving, with a strict blood/alcohol limit of
0.05 per cent. Speed limits are 130 kph (80 mph) on toll motorways,
110 kph (68 mph) on dual carriageways, 80 kph (50 mph) on other

roads and 50 kph (31 mph) in built-up areas. Speed checks are common and the police have powers to impose on-the-spot fines.

If you are involved in an accident, however minor, you must call the police immediately or your insurance will be invalid. The **Croatian Automobile Club** provides a 24-hour helpline (🛈 01 464 0800) and emergency roadside assistance (🛈 987).

ENTRY FORMALITIES

Citizens of the UK, Republic of Ireland, other EU countries, US, Canada, Australia and New Zealand need only a valid passport to enter Croatia for up to 90 days. Citizens of South Africa require a visa, available from the Croatian Embassy in Pretoria. For a full list of visa requirements and details of your nearest Croatian Embassy, see the **Ministry of Foreign Affairs** website 🅦 www.mfa.hr.

In theory, all visitors are required to register with the police within 24 hours of arrival, but this will be done for you if you are staying in a hotel.

The maximum customs allowances for adults entering Croatia are 200 cigarettes (or 50 cigars or 250 g tobacco), 2 litres of wine and 1 litre of spirits. Valuable camera equipment and laptop computers should be declared on arrival.

MONEY

Croatia's currency is the kuna (HRK or kn), divided into 100 lipa. Coins come in denominations of 1, 2, 5, 10, 20 and 50 lipa and 1, 2 and 5 kn. Banknotes, with portraits of Croatian heroes on one side and Croatian landmarks on the other, are issued in denominations of 5, 10, 20, 50, 100, 200, 500 and 1,000 kn. The kuna takes its name from the pine marten, whose pelts were used for trading in medieval times. The exchange rate fluctuates from day to day.

Hotel prices and certain other goods are increasingly quoted in euros, though it is always acceptable to pay in kuna. Major credit cards such as Visa, MasterCard and American Express are widely accepted in hotels, restaurants and shops, but you should always carry some cash for small purchases.

The easiest way of getting cash is from an ATM. You will need to use your credit or debit card with a PIN, so make sure you know it before you go. Machines accept most credit and debit cards, including Cirrus, Maestro and Plus. Instructions are given in a choice of languages.

Foreign currency and traveller's cheques can be exchanged at banks, post offices, travel agencies and hotels. The post office beside the railway station is open 24 hours a day and has currency exchange facilities.

HEALTH, SAFETY & CRIME

There are no compulsory vaccinations for Croatia. If you are taking regular medication, bring enough to last throughout your stay and bring a copy of the prescription in case you run out. Pharmacies are indicated by the word *ljekarna* and a green cross, which is lit when they are open. Some chemists in the city centre are open 24 hours a day (see page 138).

Tap water is safe to drink but mineral water tastes better. Smoking is banned on public transport, but is widespread in restaurants and bars.

The standard of public health care is high and most doctors and pharmacists speak reasonable English. EU citizens receive free emergency care and hospital treatment in Croatia on production

of their passport, but travellers from other countries must pay
and get a receipt in order to claim insurance. Non-essential
treatment may not be covered and those wishing to take a
belt-and-braces approach should consider purchasing fully
comprehensive travel insurance.

Zagreb is generally a safe city, but keep an eye out for
pickpockets on crowded trams and keep your cash and credit
cards hidden in an inside pocket or money belt. If possible, leave
valuables in a hotel safe. Rather than taking the risks inherent in
writing down lists of your credit card numbers in case of loss or
theft, it's a good idea to email such details to yourself before you
leave home. Be wary of people looking over your shoulder while
using a cash machine, and never let anyone see your PIN. If you do
encounter problems, you will find that the police are unfailingly
helpful and courteous. However, make sure your travel insurance
gives you adequate cover for lost or stolen valuables.

OPENING HOURS
Banks ◷ 07.00–19.00 Mon–Fri, 07.00–13.00 Sat
Offices ◷ 08.00–16.00 Mon–Fri
Shops ◷ 08.00–20.00 Mon–Fri, 08.00–14.00 Sat

TOILETS
There are few public facilities in Zagreb, and those that do exist,
such as at the bus and railway stations, usually make a small
charge. There are free toilets inside the Centar Kaptol shopping
mall and public toilets at Dolac market. Otherwise, your best
bet is to use a café, though it is polite to buy a drink first. Men's
toilets are usually marked *Muški* and women's are *Ženski*.

CHILDREN

Children are welcome everywhere in Zagreb. Few restaurants have special children's menus, but pizza and burgers are widely available and kids will love the ice-cream parlours on Bogovićeva with their kaleidoscopic array of colours. Items such as baby food and nappies can be bought in supermarkets. Remember that small children are particularly vulnerable to the sun, so apply plenty of sunscreen and make sure they drink lots of water on hot days.

Children under six travel free on public transport. Museums are mostly free for younger children and half-price for children of school age. Older children will enjoy the Tehnički muzej (Technical Museum, see page 134), with its gallery of planes, trains and automobiles. Included in the entry price are a tour of an

● Travelling by tram is a convenient option

underground mine, a planetarium show and free tram rides on Sundays.

Maksimir Park (see page 98) is a great space for kids, with swings, slides and pony rides. It is also home to Zagreb's zoo (see below), on a small island by a lake. The zoo has an extensive collection of animals, including bears, lions, crocodiles and penguins. Music is played to the elephant twice a day to aid relaxation (see page 98).

Tehnički muzej ⓐ Savska cesta 18 ⓣ 01 484 4050
ⓦ www.mdc.hr/tehnicki ⓛ 09.00–17.00 Tues–Fri, 09.00–13.00 Sat & Sun; mine tour: 15.00 Tues–Fri, 11.00 Sat & Sun; planetarium show: 16.00 Tues–Fri, 12.00 Sat & Sun; tram rides: 09.30 Sun ⓝ Tram: 3, 9, 12 to Tehnički muzej. Admission charge

Zoološki vrt Maksimir (Zoo) ⓐ Maksimirski perivoj bb
ⓣ 01 230 2198 ⓦ www.zoo.hr ⓛ 09.00–dusk ⓝ Tram: 4, 7, 11, 12 to Bukovačka. Admission charge

COMMUNICATIONS
Internet
High-speed internet access is widely available at internet cafés and hotels. The larger hotels have business centres, and most hotels have modem connections for laptops. Wi-Fi internet access is becoming more common. Most computers use a Croatian keyboard, so ask for help if you need it. Website and email addresses in Croatia do not use accents.
Art ⓐ Tkalčićeva 18 ⓣ 01 481 1050 ⓛ 08.00–23.00
Vip Internet Café ⓐ Trg Petra Preradovića 5 ⓣ 01 483 0089 ⓛ 08.00–23.00

TELEPHONING CROATIA

To call Croatia from abroad, dial the international access code (usually 00), followed by the country code (385), the area code (1 for Zagreb, 42 for Varaždin) and the six- or seven-digit telephone number.

TELEPHONING ABROAD

To call home from Croatia, dial the international access code (00), followed by the country code (61 for Australia, 1 for Canada or the US, 64 for New Zealand, 44 for the UK, 353 for Ireland), the area code (minus the initial 0, in the case of the UK) and the rest of the number.

Phones

There are public telephones on almost every street corner. Phones use magnetic phonecards, which can be bought at tobacconists and kiosks for 30, 50 or 100 kn. Calls to the UK and Europe cost around 3 kn per minute, so the cheapest card will last about ten minutes. You can also make metered calls from post offices. It is best to avoid making international calls from your hotel as the charges are likely to be excessive.

Most European and North American mobile phones will work in Croatia, provided you have set up international access with your network operator. The two main networks in Croatia are VIP and T-Com. If you are going to be making a lot of calls, consider buying a local SIM card for your phone.

Post

You can find yellow postboxes all over Zagreb. Stamps can be purchased from newsagents and kiosks as well as post offices. The main post office is close to Trg bana Jelačića at ⓐ Jurišićeva 13 🕒 07.00–21.00 Mon–Fri, 08.00–15.00 Sat.

The post office beside the railway station is open 24 hours a day. Letters and postcards take around five days to Europe and two weeks to North America.

ELECTRICITY

The electrical current is supplied at 220 volts. Standard continental two-pin plugs are used, so British visitors will need an adaptor and visitors from the US will need a transformer for appliances operating on 110 volts.

TRAVELLERS WITH DISABILITIES

Attitudes to people with disabilities in Croatia have been shaped by the war, which left many people with permanent disability. Although Zagreb is not the easiest city to get around in a wheelchair and many older buildings are still not fully accessible, visitors with disabilities will usually be offered help and treated with respect. Old-style buses and trams are gradually being replaced by new, low-floor vehicles, though most trams are still not accessible for wheelchairs. Visitors with disabilities and their travelling companions can use a free **dial-a-ride taxi service** (☎ 01 299 5956), which must be booked at least one day in advance.

TOURIST INFORMATION

Tourist Information Office ⓐ Trg bana Jelačića 11 ☏ 01 481 4051
ⓦ www.zagreb-touristinfo.hr ⏰ 08.30–20.00 Mon–Fri,
09.00–17.00 Sat, 10.00–14.00 Sun

Tourist information is available from April to October on
a dedicated phone line from **Croatian Angels** (☏ 062 999999).

For information on Croatia before you go, contact the
Croatian National Tourist Office in the UK (☏ 020 8563 7979)
or see their website (ⓦ www.croatia.hr).

BACKGROUND READING

Black Lamb and Grey Falcon by Rebecca West is a classic
travelogue of a journey through Yugoslavia in the 1930s.
Croatia: A Nation Forged in War by Marcus Tanner is a
comprehensive and readable account of Croatian history.
How We Survived Communism and Even Laughed by Slavenka
Drakulić is one Croatian woman's wry and witty observations
on life in Communist Yugoslavia.
They Would Never Hurt a Fly by Slavenka Drakulić describes the
madness that gripped Yugoslavia during the 1990s.

Emergencies

EMERGENCY NUMBERS
In an emergency call:
Ambulance ❶ 94
Fire brigade ❶ 93
Police ❶ 92
General emergency number ❶ 112

MEDICAL SERVICES
Emergency dentist
Stomatološka poliklinika Zagreb ❸ Perkovčeva 3 ❶ 01 482 8488

Hospitals
Emergency medical and hospital treatment is provided free of charge for EU citizens, but non-essential treatment and prescriptions must be paid for. The following hospitals have English-speaking doctors and are open 24 hours a day:
Klinička bolnica Dubrava ❸ Avenija Gojka Šuška 6, Dubrava ❶ 01 290 2444
Klinika za traumatologiju ❸ Draškovićeva 19 ❶ 01 469 7000

Pharmacies
These centrally located pharmacies are open 24 hours a day:
Gradska ljekarna ❸ Ilica 301 ❶ 01 375 0321
Gradska ljekarna ❸ Trg bana Jelačića 3 ❶ 01 481 6198

POLICE
Go to your nearest police station if you have anything lost or

EMERGENCY PHRASES

Fire!	**Stop!**	**Help!**
Požar!	Stani!	Upomoć!
Po-zhar!	*Stah-ni!*	*'U-po-motch!*

Call an ambulance/a doctor/the police/the fire service!
Pozovite hitnu pomoć/liječnika/policiju/vatrogasce!
*Po-'zo-vi-te hit-nu po-motch/'li-yech-ni-ka/po-'li-tsi-yu/
va-tro-'gas-tse!*

stolen. You will need to get an official police report to make
a claim on your insurance policy. You will need to get in touch
with your consulate or embassy immediately if your passport
is stolen.
Central police station ⓐ Petrinjska 30 ☎ 01 456 3127

EMBASSIES & CONSULATES
Contact your embassy immediately if your passport is lost or
stolen, or if you are in trouble with the police.
Australia ⓐ Centar Kaptol, Nova ves 11 ☎ 01 489 1200
Canada ⓐ Prilaz Đure Deželića 4 ☎ 01 488 1200
New Zealand ⓐ Vlaška 50A ☎ 01 461 2060
Republic of Ireland ⓐ Miramarska 23 ☎ 01 631 0025
UK ⓐ Ivana Lučića 4 ☎ 01 600 9100
US ⓐ Thomasa Jeffersona 2 ☎ 01 661 2200